LIFE WITH GOD

ALSO BY RICHARD FOSTER

Celebration of Discipline

Money, Sex and Power

Prayer

LIFE
WITH
GOD

—

Richard J. Foster
with
Kathryn A. Helmers

HODDER &
STOUGHTON

First published in Great Britain in 2008 by Hodder & Stoughton
An Hachette Livre UK company

1

Copyright © Renovaré Inc., 2008

A CIP catalogue record for this title is available from the British Library

ISBN 978 0 340 95494 2

Typeset in Granjon by Palimpsest Book Production Limited Grangemouth, Stirlingshire

Printed and bound by Clays Ltd, St Ives plc

Hodder & Stoughton policy is to use papers that are natural, renewable and recyclable products and made from wood grown in sustainable forests. The logging and manufacturing processes are expected to conform to the environmental regulations of the country of origin.

Hodder & Stoughton Ltd
338 Euston Road
London NW1 3BH

www.hodderfaith.com

Contents

Part 3
UNDERSTANDING THE MEANS

A Word to the Reader

This book grows out of a deep, heartfelt concern that you and I and all peoples everywhere might discover the *life with God* to which the Bible witnesses so eloquently. This concern has its roots in the five years of intensive work that I (along with many others) did to produce the Renovaré *Spiritual Formation Bible*. As we worked intensively with the biblical witness, we all were profoundly struck by two great realities.

First, we found that the unity of the Bible is discovered in the development of life *with* God as a reality on earth, centered in the person of Jesus. Through Scripture we heard God whispering down through the centuries: "I am *with* you!" "I am *with* you!" "I am *with* you!" Then, we heard God asking a question that searches the human person to the depths: "Are you willing to be *with* Me?" The Scripture reveals that saying "yes" to this invitation thrusts human beings into life *with* God . . . daily . . . hourly . . . moment by moment.

Second, the biblical witness showed us how this with-God life works itself out in every conceivable way and in every conceivable circumstance. We learned how God was *with* God's people in individual communion: *with* Adam, *with* Eve, *with* Enoch, *with* Noah. Next, under Abraham we came to understand how God was *with* God's people in the development of family life. We followed the story as it continued on through the Exodus into the Promised Land and the building of a nation, in the people's rebellion, and ultimately into their exile. Through it all, God remained *with* God's people. Then we saw how God brought about the restoration and, in the fullness of time, we witnessed the coming of Immanuel. Ultimately, in the formation of the church we saw the creation of an all-inclusive community of loving persons, with God at its very center as its prime Sustainer and most glorious Inhabitant.

We perceived this "with-God" life as a cosmic principle that God has used all along in creation and redemption and restoration, extending out beyond human history into eternity.[1] We also came to the realization that this strange and eccentric Bible story is allover autobiographic of us. Just as God kept saying in ancient times, so God keeps saying today: "I am *with* you in all the love and terror and pity and pain and wonder that is your life. I am *with* you. Are you willing to be *with* Me?"

Our deep concern for the Bible as the foundational text for Christian spiritual formation continues in this little book, which has been developed to invite us into a deeper and more authentic life *with God*. It seeks to illuminate *The Immanuel Principle*—the dynamic of spiritual transformation intertwining divine action and human reaction—in all of human experience, from the stories of biblical characters through the generations of Christian tradition to our own lives today. Always, the purpose of such understanding is not that we will become proficient in our Bible knowledge. Rather, it is that we will be enabled to live out of this "life that is life indeed" into ongoing discipleship to Jesus in such a way that our hearts and minds are progressively transformed into the very nature of the heart and mind of God (1 Tim. 6:19).

As the primary way of becoming intentional participants in this glorious vision, we explore the scripturally based, time-honored practices of the Spiritual Disciplines, which open the door to becoming more like the God into whose presence and life they usher us.

THE HIDDEN RESERVOIR

As we allow the Scripture to lead us into the process of transformation, we discover that it is not a matter of religious beliefs and behavior. No—we are entering into a dynamic, pulsating life! Our trusted friend the Apostle Paul writes, "There is therefore now no condemnation for those who are in Christ Jesus. For the law of spirit of **life** in Christ Jesus has set you free from the law of sin and death" (Rom. 8:1–2, emphasis added). Paul is here using a very specific word to identify the secret of our life "hidden with Christ in God" (Col.3:3): *zoë*, the eternal, uncreated life that originates in God alone.

Scripture identifies two types of life: *bios*, the physical, created life; and *zoë*, the spiritual, eternal life. Likewise, there are two types of death: *teleute*, physical death; and *thanatos*, spiritual death. Thus, it is entirely possible for a person to be physically alive (*bios*) while spiritually dead (*thanatos*). But the salvation that is in Jesus Christ immerses us into the hidden reservoir of divine love and power. Jesus declares, "I am come that they might have life [*zoë*], and that they might have it more abundantly" (John

10:10, KJV). In his first Epistle John writes, "God gave us eternal life [*zoë*], and this life [*zoë*] is in his Son" (1 John 5:11). And Paul writes, "For if while we were enemies, we were reconciled to God through the death of his Son, much more surely, having been reconciled, will we be saved by his life [*zoë*]" (Rom. 5:10). Life. Life. Life. It is all about life: imperishable, unceasing *zoë*.

But we must seek this life out, pursue it, turn into it because there is also a principle of death within us, stemming from the fall. Therefore, we must be constantly saying "yes" to life and "no" to death. We must always be discerning life-giving actions and attitudes from those that are death-giving. This is why the Bible is such a help to us; it is regularly fleshing these things out in the rough-and-tumble of real-life situations. Scripture makes clear to us precisely how this "with God" life works in all the circumstances of human existence, both for individuals and for groups, both in specific historical periods and throughout all times.

A DWELLING PLACE FOR GOD

Now, all this struggling and learning to live "with God" has a rock-solid purpose to it: to transform us into the likeness and character of Jesus. God's everlasting intent for human life is that we should be in every aspect a dwelling place for God. We are, in God's time and in God's way, to be set free from fornication and impurity and licentiousness and idolatry and sorcery and enmities and strife and jealousy and anger and quarrels and dissensions and factions and envy and drunkenness and carousing and things like these (Gal. 5:19–21). Conversely, we are, in God's time and in God's way, to take on the spiritual fruit of love and joy and peace and patience and kindness and generosity and faithfulness and gentleness and self control (Gal. 5:22–23).

Heaven is most certainly an important part of this "with God life." This life is, after all, eternal. Hence, we want to become the kind of person inwardly so that when we do get to heaven we will want to stay there. Our feelings and passions and affections will have been so transformed that we will feel right at home in heaven. Nor does this transforming process have to wait for heaven. Oh, no, it begins now ... today. Entering a "with God life" baptizes us into the milieu of the Holy Spirit. Everything around us becomes scented with the fragrance of heaven, and this touches us in ways we do not fully understand. We begin to "turn, turn, turn 'til we turn round right," as the old Shaker hymn puts it.

This is a subterranean, inner process of transformation. The heart is deeply and surely healed and restored and redirected by God alone. Old affections of hate and guile and envy are simply gone. New affections of faith and hope and love are in their place. Love and joy and peace in the Holy Spirit seem to flow from us; simply, naturally.

How, you may ask, does such a transformed life come into being? Vision. Intention. Means. These three operating under the grace of God will immerse us in a life that is penetrated throughout by love, that responds to everything in the light of God's overriding governance for good, that has the power to overcome evil with Christlikeness. We will increasingly live a "with-God life."

Richard J. Foster
Christmas Eve, 2007

Part 1

Catching the Vision

Christians feed on Scripture. Holy Scripture nurtures the holy community as food nurtures the human body. Christians don't simply learn or study or use Scripture; we assimilate it, take it into our lives in such a way that it gets metabolized into acts of love, cups of cold water, missions into all the world, healing and evangelism and justice in Jesus' name, hands raised in adoration of the Father, feet washed in company with the Son.

—Eugene Peterson,
Eat This Book

1

Seeing the Bible Afresh

I am about to do a new thing;
    now it springs forth, do you not perceive it?
I will make a way in the wilderness
    and rivers in the desert.
                                —Isaiah 43:19

God has given us a written revelation of who God is and of what God's purposes are for humanity. And God has chosen to accomplish this great work through the People of God on earth. This written revelation now resides as a massive fact at the heart of human history. There is, simply, no book that is remotely close to achieving the significance and influence of the Bible. It is truly The Book *(hay Biblos)*.

But the intrinsic power and greatness of the Bible does not make it easy for us to receive the life it offers. The average "Bible consumer," publishing research tells us, owns nine Bibles and is looking for more. This is mute but powerful testimony to a deep and abiding sense of *lack*—a sense that we have not really achieved a grasp of the Bible that is adequate to our needs.

In point of fact, we can often use the Bible in ways that stifle spiritual life or even destroy the soul. This happened to any number of people who walked with Jesus, heard him teach, and saw him exercise the power of the kingdom of God. For many, their very study of the Scriptures prevented them from recognizing who he was and from putting their confidence in him (John 5:39–47). And later, Peter speaks in very grim terms of how people can "twist" Scripture "to their own destruction" (2 Pet. 3:16).

Is it possible that this still happens today? Sadly, we must admit that it does. Think of the multiplied millions of people who say, sincerely, that the Bible is *the* guide to life but who still starve to death in the presence of its spiritual feast. This tragic situation is obvious from the usual effects (or lack of effects) that the study of the Bible has in the daily lives of people, even among those who speak most highly of it.

THE SOURCE OF THE PROBLEM

The source of the problem is rooted in the two most common objectives people have for studying the Bible. The first is the practice of studying the Bible for information or knowledge alone. This may include information about particular facts or historical events, or knowledge of general truths or doctrines, or even knowledge of how others are mistaken in their religious views, beliefs, and practices.

We know from experience how knowledge can make people arrogant—even knowledge of the Bible and of God. It is not surprising, then, that study that focuses on knowledge alone does not lead to life transformation, which is the real human need. No wonder we who love the Bible keep buying more editions of it, hoping to obtain what we know in our hearts is there for us.

The second common objective people often have for studying the Bible is to find some formula that will solve the pressing need of the moment. Thus we seek out lists of specific passages that speak to particular needs rather than seeking whole-life discipleship to Jesus. To be sure, these needs are important, desperately so when we are trapped in the harsh realities of life. They can involve anything from needs for comfort or forgiveness, to physical healing, to conformity to a particular denominational or political persuasion, to special endowments or gifts of the Spirit, to works of social liberation. But in the end they always have to do with being "a good citizen," "a good spouse," or "a good something else"—perhaps even with being "a good Christian" by certain interpretations.

What we must face up to about these two common objectives for studying the Bible is that they always leave us or someone else *in charge*. They are, in fact, ways of trying to control what comes out of the Bible rather than entering the process of the transformation of our whole person and of our whole life into *Christlikeness*.

If we want to receive from the Bible the life "with God" that is portrayed *in* the Bible, we must be prepared to have our dearest and most fundamental assumptions about ourselves and our associations called into question. We must read humbly and in a constant attitude of repentance. Only in this way can we gain a thorough and practical grasp of the spiritual riches that God has made available to all humanity in his written Word. Only in this way can we keep from transforming The Book into a Catholic Bible, an Orthodox Bible, a Protestant Bible, an "Ours Is More Accurate than Yours" Bible.

What will enable us to avoid this soul-crushing result?

THE SUPERNATURAL POWER OF LOVE

Jesus founded on earth a new type of community, and in it and through him, love—God-given *agape* love—came down to live with power on earth. Now, it is this God-given *agape* love that transforms our lives and gives us true spiritual substance as persons. Suppose, then, we simply agreed that the proper outcome of studying the Bible is growth in the supernatural power of love: love of God and of all people?

We could call this The First Corinthians 13 Test: "If I . . . understand all mysteries and all knowledge, and if I have all faith, so as to remove mountains, but do not have love, I am nothing" (verse 2). And so the test of whether or not we have really gotten the point of the Bible would then be the quality of love that we show.

Knowledge of the Bible and its teachings would, of course, continue to be of great value, but only insofar as it leads to greater love: to greater appropriation of God's love for us and for us to have greater love for God, others, and ourselves.

When we turn to Scripture in this way, our reason for "knowing" the Bible and everything it teaches would be that we might love more and know more of love. We would experience this love not as an abstraction but as a practical reality by which we are possessed. And since all those who love through and through obey the law, we would become ever more obedient to Jesus Christ and his Abba Father.

Regarding the Bible, then, perhaps the most basic question is: Shall we try to control the Bible, that is, try to make it "come out right," or shall we simply seek to release its life into our lives and into our world? Shall we try to "tilt" it this way or that, or shall we give it complete freedom to "tilt" us as it will?

Can we surrender freely to the life we see in the Bible, or must we remain in control of that life, only selectively endorsing it so far as we find it proper and safe from our "perspective"? Can we trust the living water that flows from Christ through the Bible, open ourselves to it and open it up into the world as best we can, and then get out of its way? This is the goal of reading the Bible for spiritual transformation.

LIFE WITH GOD: THE IMMANUEL PRINCIPLE

The Bible is all about human life "*with God.*" It is about how God has made this "with" life possible and will bring it to pass. In fact, the name *Immanuel,* meaning "God is with us," is the title given to the one and only Redeemer because it refers to God's everlasting intent for human life—namely, that we should be in every aspect a dwelling place of God. Indeed, the unity of the Bible is discovered in the development of life with God as a reality on earth, centered in the person of Jesus. We might call this *The Immanuel Principle* of life.

This dynamic, pulsating, *with-God* life is on nearly every page of the Bible. To the point of redundancy we hear that *God* is *with* people: with Abraham, with Moses, with Esther, with David, with Isaiah and Jeremiah and Amos and Micah and Haggai and Malachi, with Mary, with Peter, with James and John, with Paul and Barnabas, with Priscilla and Aquila, with Lydia, Timothy, Epaphroditus, Phoebe, and a host of others too numerous to name. These varied stories form a mosaic illustrating how the "with" life works in all circumstances of human existence, both in specific historical periods and through all times.

This mosaic suggests a beautiful design for the way in which we view the Scriptures. From Genesis to Revelation we learn that The Immanuel Principle is, after all, a *cosmic* principle that God has used all along in creation and redemption. It alone serves to guide human life aright on earth now and even illuminates the future of the universe. It is the wellsprings of the river of life flowing through the Bible, surging with the gracious word of God to all humankind—"I am with you." This river pours into the thirsty wastelands of the human soul, inviting us to enter with its insistent call, "Will you be with Me?" Now, once we decide to surrender freely to this river of life, we must learn how to see into the divine Life within the Bible, and increasingly receive that Life as our own, not just for us but for the sake of the world God so loves.

NURTURING THE INTENTION

God not only originated the Bible through human authorship; God remains with it always. It is God's book. No one owns it but God. It is the loving heart of God made visible and plain. And receiving this message of exquisite love is the great privilege of all who long for life with God. Reading and studying and memorizing and meditating upon Scripture have always been the foundation of the Christian Disciplines. All of the Disciplines are built upon Scripture. Our practice of the Spiritual Disciplines is kept on course by our immersion in Scripture. And so it is, we come to see, that this reading and studying and memorizing and meditating is totally in the service of "the life that really is life" (1 Tim. 6:19). We long with all our hearts to know for ourselves this with-God kind of life that Jesus brings in all its fullness.

And the Bible has been given to help us. God has so superintended the writing of Scripture that it serves as a most reliable guide for our own spiritual formation. But as in its authorship, so in its presentation to the world, God uses human action. So we must consider how we can ourselves come to the Bible and also how we can present it to all peoples in a way that does not destroy the soul but inducts it into the eternal kind of life.

We begin by opening our lives in Christian community to the influx of God's life, and by experientially finding, day-to-day, how to let Jesus Christ live in every dimension of our being. We can gather regularly in little groups of two or more to encourage one another to discover the footprints of God in our daily existence and to venture out *with God* into areas where we have previously walked alone or not at all.

But the aim is not external conformity, whether to doctrine or deed, but the re-formation of the inner self—of the spiritual core, the place of thought and feeling, of will and character. "Behold," cries the psalmist, "you desire truth in the inward being; therefore teach me wisdom in my secret heart. . . . Create in me a clean heart, O God, and put a new and right spirit within me" (Ps. 51:6, 10). It is the "inner person" that "is being *renewed [renovare]* day by day" (2 Cor. 4:16).

While the many Christian traditions have differed over the details of spiritual formation, they all come out at the same place: the transformation of the person into Christlikeness. "Spiritual formation" is the process of transforming the inner reality of the self (the inward being of the psalmist) in such a way that the overall life with *God* seen in the Bible naturally and freely comes to pass in us. Our inner world (the secret heart) becomes the home of Jesus, by his initiative and our response. As a result, our interior world becomes increasingly like the inner self of Jesus, and, therefore, the natural source of the words and deeds that are characteristic of him. By his enabling presence we come to "let the same mind be in you that was in Christ Jesus" (Phil. 2:5).

This, then, provides the answer to our question about how we can present the Bible to human beings in a way that does not destroy the soul, but inducts it into the eternal kind of life. We simply do all we can to see clearly the Life that burns brightly on the pages of the Bible and to learn, by practical steps, how we can bring our entire life into that Life. An intelligent, humble, careful, intensive, straightforward reading of the Bible will direct us into Life in the kingdom of God.

READING WITH UNDERSTANDING

In seeking to discover this with-God life it is helpful to read the Bible in four distinct ways.

First, we read the Bible literally. Reading from cover to cover, internalizing its life-giving message. By reading the whole of Scripture, we begin to apprehend its force and power. We enter into the original dynamics and drama of Scripture: struggling with Abraham over the offering up of the son of promise; puzzling with Job at the tragedies of life; rejoicing with Moses at Israel's release from the house of bondage; weeping with Jeremiah "for the slain of my poor people" (Jer. 9:11); bowing in awe with Mary at the messianic promise.

Second, we read the Bible in context. This means allowing the way in which the author originally depicted life with God to establish the standard for understanding our life with God today. We read with a firm determination to discover the intent of the original author, and then allow that intent to control our comprehension of the passage. All this helps us grasp the way God continues to shape human life today.

Third, we read the Bible in conversation with itself. In other words, we seek to understand how the whole of Scripture gives structure and meaning to each of its parts. The unfolding drama of Scripture often raises puzzling questions that are resolved only when more obscure and difficult passages are held under the light of clearer, more straightforward passages. In biblical interpretation, systematic passages interpret incidental passages; universal passages interpret local ones; didactic passages interpret symbolic ones. In this way the whole Bible guides us into a better understanding of its particular parts.

Fourth, Christians read the Bible in conversation with the historic witness of the People of God. The Church learned from the Synagogue that it is the community that reads the Bible. This, in part, is what we mean when we speak of "the communion of saints." Christians throughout the centuries help us understand the nature of life with God and provide insight and discernment that enrich our own spiritual life. So we read the Bible in conversation with Origen and Jerome, Augustine of Hippo and Hildegard of Bingen, John Chrysostom and John Calvin, Martin Luther and Richard Baxter, Watchman Nee and Sundar Singh— and many others, including wise and mature interpreters of Scripture today. This corporate reading of the Bible illuminates for us the multifaceted ways The Immanuel Principle is experienced in ordinary life.

READING WITH THE HEART

Finally, as we approach the Bible it is helpful to slow down, breathe deeply, and read with the heart. Now, this "reading with the heart" way of approaching the sacred text has a very long and time-honored history among the People of God. It even has a name, *lectio divina,* Latin for divine or spiritual reading.

What does *lectio divina* mean? Well, it means *listening* to the text of Scripture—really listening; listening yielded and still. It means *submitting* to the text of Scripture; allowing its message to flow into us rather than our attempting to master it. It means *reflecting* on the text of Scripture; permitting ourselves to become fully engaged—both mind and heart—by the drama of the passage. It means *praying* the text of Scripture; letting the biblical reality of this with-God life give rise to our heart cry of gratitude or confession or complaint or petition. It means *applying* the text of Scripture; seeing how God's Holy Word provides a personal word for our life circumstances. And, it means *obeying* the text of Scripture; turning, always turning, from our wicked ways and into the way everlasting (Ps. 139:23–24).

UNDERSTANDING THE MEANS

The with-God kind of life that we see in the Bible is the very life to which we are called. It is, in fact, exactly the life Jesus is referring to when he declares, "I am come that they might have life, and that they might have it more abundantly" (John 10:10, KJV). It is a life of unhurried peace and power. It is solid. It is serene. It is simple. It is radiant. It takes no time, though it permeates all of our time.

But such a life does not simply fall into our hands. Frankly, it is no more automatic for us than it was for those luminaries who walk across the pages of our Bible. There is a God-ordained means to becoming the kind of persons and the kind of communities that can fully and joyfully enter into such abundant living. And these "means" involve us in a process of intentionally "training . . . in godliness" (1 Tim. 4:7). This is the purpose of the *Disciplines* of the spiritual life. Indeed, Scripture itself is the primary means for the discovery, instruction, and practice of the Spiritual Disciplines, which bring us all the more fully into the *with God* life.

The Spiritual Disciplines, then, are the God-ordained means by which each of us is enabled to bring the individualized power-pack we all possess—the human body—and place it before God as "a living sacrifice" (Rom. 12:1). It is the way we go about training in the spiritual life. By means of this process we become, through time and experience, the kind of person who naturally and freely expresses "love, joy, peace, patience, kindness, generosity, faithfulness, gentleness, and self-control" (Gal. 5:22–23).

MANY AND VARIED

What are these Spiritual Disciplines of which we are speaking? Oh, they are many and varied: fasting and prayer, study and service, submission and solitude, confession and worship, meditation and silence, simplicity, frugality, secrecy, sacrifice, celebration, and the like. We see such Spiritual Disciplines cropping up repeatedly in the Bible as the way God's People trained themselves and were trained by God toward godliness. And not only in the Bible; the saints down through history, even spilling over into our own time, have all practiced these ways of "growing in grace" (see 2 Pet. 3:18).

Biblical examples abound of individual listings and common groupings of Spiritual Disciplines in much the same way that athletes have a basic regimen of training for particular sports. And this makes perfect sense since these biblical personages were (and we are) the *athletae dei*, the athletes of God. As the athletes of God they trained (and we train) to participate fully and freely in this with-God kind of life. The Psalms virtually sing of the meditations of the People of God: "My eyes are awake before each watch of the night, that I may meditate on your promise" (Ps. 119:148). The psalm that introduces the entire Psalter calls us to emulate those whose "delight is in the law of the LORD, and on his law they meditate day and night" (Ps. 1:2). Daniel "turned to the LORD God" with prayer, supplication, fasting, and confession (Dan. 9:3). Jesus, "in the morning, while it was still very dark . . . got up and went out to a deserted place" (Mark 1:35). The Christians at Antioch were "worshiping the Lord and fasting" when they received Divine guidance to commission Paul and Barnabas to their missionary task (Acts 13:1–3). And on it goes.

We can see this process not only in the Bible but also in the stories of God's people throughout the ages. Perhaps you have read or heard of *The Spiritual Exercises* of Ignatius of Loyola or Teresa of Avila's *Interior Castle* or Jeremy Taylor's *Holy Living and Dying* or William Law's *A Serious Call to a Devout and Holy Life*. These writings, and many others like them, all discuss Disciplines of the spiritual life for training in righteousness.

So groupings and patterns of Spiritual Disciplines abound. But, we should never look for some exhaustive list of the Spiritual Disciplines. Nor for any "formula for blessedness." No, this interactive life "with God" is far too dynamic for that.

Now, through all this we need not fear. We are not left to our own devices. God is with us. Christ is our ever-living Teacher. The Spirit will guide and direct. Wise Christian counsel abounds in both Scripture and among loving and mature friends. We will be taught which response is right and when. And which Disciplines are needful and when. Our only task is to listen. And obey.

THE PRINCIPLE OF INDIRECTION

When we engage in the Spiritual Disciplines, we are seeking the righteousness of the kingdom of God through "indirection." You see, we cannot by direct effort make ourselves into the kind of people who can live fully alive to God. Only God can accomplish this in us. Only God can incline our heart toward him. Only God can reprogram the deeply ingrained habit patterns of sin that constantly predispose us toward evil and transform them into even more deeply ingrained habit patterns of "righteousness and peace and joy in the Holy Spirit" (Rom. 14:17). And God freely and graciously invites us to participate in this transforming process. But not on our own.

We do not, for example, become humble merely by trying to become humble. Action on our own would make us all the more proud of our humility. No, we instead train with Spiritual Disciplines appropriate to our need. In this particular example that would most surely involve learning numerous acts of service for others that would incline us toward the good of all people. This indirect action will place us—body, mind, and spirit—before God as a living sacrifice. God then takes this little offering of ourselves and in a divine time and in a divine way produces in us things far greater than we could ever ask or think—in this case a life growing in and overflowing with the grace of humility. It is, to repeat, the righteousness of the kingdom of God by indirection.

WHAT IS A SPIRITUAL DISCIPLINE?

Now, to move forward in this life, we must understand clearly what a Spiritual Discipline is in the first place. *A Spiritual Discipline is an intentionally directed action by which we do what we* can *do in order to receive from God the ability (or power) to do what we cannot do by direct effort.* It is not in us, for example, to love our enemies. We might even go out and try very hard to love our enemies, but we will fail miserably. Always. This strength, this power to love our enemies—that is, to genuinely and unconditionally love those who curse us and despitefully use us—is simply not within our natural abilities. We cannot do it by ourselves. Ever.

But this fact of life does not mean that we do nothing. Far from it! Instead, by an act of the will we choose to take up Disciplines of the spiritual life that we can do. These Disciplines are all actions of body, mind, and spirit that are within our power to do. Not always and not perfectly, to be sure. But they are things we can do. By choice. By choosing actions of *fasting* we can learn experientially that we do not live by bread alone but by every word that proceeds from the mouth of God (Deut. 8:3; Luke 4:4). By choosing actions of *study* we can learn how the mind takes on an order conforming to the order upon which it concentrates, which is precisely why we seek to turn our mind toward all things "true, whatever is honorable, whatever is just, whatever is pure, whatever is pleasing, whatever is commendable, if there is any excellence and if there is anything worthy of praise, think about these things" (Phil. 4:8). By choosing actions of *solitude* we can become intimately acquainted with the many things that control us so that we can be set free from them by the power of God (Mark 6:31). And so forth.

Now, the Spiritual Disciplines in and of themselves have no merit whatsoever. They possess no righteousness, contain no rectitude. Their purpose—their only purpose—is to place us before God. After that they have come to the end of their tether. But it is enough. Then the grace of God steps in and takes this simple offering of ourselves and creates out of it the kind of person who embodies the goodness of God; indeed, a person who can come to the place of truly loving even enemies.

Again, Spiritual Disciplines involve doing what we *can* do to receive from God the power to do what we cannot do. And God graciously uses this process to produce in us the kind of person who automatically will do what needs to be done when it needs to be done.

This ability to do what needs to be done when it needs to be done is the true freedom in life. Freedom comes not from the absence of restraint but from the presence of discipline. Only the disciplined gymnast is free to score a perfect ten on the parallel bars. Only the disciplined violinist is free to play Paganini's "Caprices." This, of course, is true in all of life, but it is never more true than in the spiritual life. When we are on the spot, when we find ourselves in the midst of the crisis, it is too late. Training in the Spiritual Disciplines is the God-ordained means for forming and transforming the human personality so that in the emergency we can be "response-able"—able to respond appropriately.

GRACE, GRACE, AND MORE GRACE

It is vitally important for us to see all this spiritual training in the context of the work and action of God's grace. As the great Apostle reminds us, "it is God who is at work in you, enabling you both to will and to work for his good pleasure" (Phil. 2:13). This, you see, is no "works righteousness," as it is sometimes called. Even our desiring of this with-God kind of life is an action of grace; it is "prevenient grace," say the theologians. You see, we are not just saved by grace; we live by grace. And we pray by grace and fast by grace and study by grace and serve by grace and worship by grace. *All the Disciplines are permeated by the enabling grace of God.*

But do not misunderstand; there *are* things for us to do. Daily. Grace never means inaction or total passivity. In ordinary life we will encounter multiple moments of decision where we must engage the will saying, "Yes!" to God's will and to God's way as the People of God have been challenged throughout history. The opposite of grace is works, but not effort.

"Works" have to do with earning, and there simply is nothing any of us can do to earn God's love or acceptance. And, of course, we don't have to. God already loves us utterly and perfectly, and our complete acceptance is the free gift of God through Jesus Christ our Lord. In God's amazing grace we live and move and have our being. But if we ever hope to "grow in grace," we will find ourselves engaging in effort of the most strenuous kind. As Jesus says, we are to "*strive* to enter through the narrow door" (Luke 13:24, emphasis added). And Peter urges us to "make every *effort* to support your faith with goodness, and goodness with knowledge, and knowledge with self-control, and self-control with endurance, and endurance with godliness, and godliness with mutual affection, and mutual affection with love" (2 Pet. 1:5–7, emphasis added).

GO AND DO LIKEWISE

As you read the Bible, be on the lookout for the formation— indeed, the transformation—of those who walk across its pages. Pay attention even to those who resist God's initiatives and are never really formed into Christlikeness: the Esaus and the

Balaams, the Ahabs and the Manassehs, the Jezebels, and the Judases. Note the struggles. Look for the intention, or the lack of intention. Observe the various and sundry Spiritual Disciplines used. Watch the movement back and forth: defiance and obedience, rebellion and submission, loyalty and unfaithfulness.

Give special attention to those who do come through on the other side—albeit with many slips and falls. Note their joy. Their peace. Their strength. Their love. They are the ones who are experiencing ever more fully The Immanuel Principle, the with-God life. Then, go and do likewise.

2

Entering the World of the Bible

> You search the scriptures because you think that in them
> you have eternal life; and it is they that testify on my
> behalf.
>
> —John 5:39

The Bible is like a vast geographical basin in which tributary
streams feed into the currents of a parent river on its course to
the ocean. The riverbanks are interspersed with openings where
the tributaries join the larger body of water. These points, scattered all along the way from the sources of the river to its mouth,
are places of surging turbulence, fierce and joyful, where the
swirling eddies of intermingling currents make it no longer possible to distinguish smaller waters from the mighty flow gathering them into itself. This is how the Bible creates meeting places
for human spirit and Divine Spirit.

When we sit down with the Bible and open its pages, seeking
to draw near to God, what kind of inner attitude is most helpful
for ushering us into the refreshing spiritual waters for which we
thirst? This is not a matter of the mechanics of Bible study, or

whether to start with Genesis, or the Gospel of John, or daily readings coupling excerpts from the Psalms and Proverbs.[2] No, it is much more a matter of how to tune mind, heart, and soul for reading the Bible as spiritual practice, so that we might grow in the supernatural love of God.

Reading the Bible for interior transformation is a far different endeavor than reading the Bible for historical knowledge, literary appreciation, or religious instruction. In the latter case we learn head knowledge; in the former, heart knowledge. To allow the Bible to infiltrate us with the Life God offers—piercing us like a two-edged sword dividing "soul from spirit, joints from marrow . . . [judging] the thoughts and intentions of the heart" (Heb. 4:12)—we must bring to the Bible our whole selves, expectantly, attentively, and humbly.

ENTER EXPECTANTLY

First, we bring our lives to the Life within the Bible by coming *expectantly*—"Holy Expectancy" is what the ancient writers called it. The human authors of Scripture were part of another era, but there is a Living Author waiting to meet us. Reading the Bible for spiritual transformation is a not a one-sided endeavor: it is a dialogue of human spirit and Holy Spirit.

What is our part, practically speaking, in this dialogue? Well, there is a difference between simply being in the same room with others versus truly being *present* to them. It is a hollow feeling to be in the company of someone with whom we long to have a satisfying personal exchange, only to watch hope dissolve as the time together is drained by superficial chatter or surface distractions.

Does God feel disappointment when we leaf through the Bible absentmindedly, as if scanning the sports page for scores on our favorite teams or checking the news section for headlines and on-sale advertisements? "I wish that you were either cold or hot," said the angel to the church in Laodicea. "So, because you are lukewarm, and neither cold nor hot, I am about to spit you out of my mouth" (Rev. 3:15–16). This is not to say that we should read the Bible out of guilt, or to reduce God to human level by senti-mentalizing divine emotions. But our appetite for the Divine can be whetted by knowing that God is longing for us to be present to the Spirit, just as the Spirit is present to us.

In the same passage warning against lukewarmness, the angel brings this word from God to the Laodiceans ... and to us: "Listen! I am standing at the door, knocking; if you hear my voice and open the door, I will come in to you and eat with you, and you with me" (Rev. 3:20). From start to finish, God is always the initiator of relationship with us: creating relationship, pursu-ing relationship, repairing relationship, empowering relation-ship, consummating relationship. We have freedom to respond as we choose, but first and foremost it is always *God* who acts. The Apostle John wrote, "In this is love, not that we loved God but that he loved us ..." (1 John 4:10).

We can bring heart, mind, and soul to the Bible by expecting God to meet us there. This does not mean, of course, that God will always meet us in the same way or to the same degree of in-tensity each time we read or study the Bible. It does mean that we can always expect the living Word to meet us through the written words of the Bible.

It is important to distinguish between the Bible as the written Word of God and the living God who is revealed through the Bible. Dallas Willard makes this distinction clear:

> [While] the Bible is the written Word of God, the word of God is not simply the Bible. . . . The Bible is the Word of God in its unique *written* form. But the Bible is not Jesus Christ, who is the *living* Word. The Bible was not born of a virgin, crucified, resurrected and elevated to the right hand of the Father.
>
> Neither is the Bible the word of God that is settled eternally in the heavens as the psalmist says (Ps. 119:89), expressing itself in the order of nature (Ps. 19:1–4). The Bible is not the word of God that, in the book of Acts, expanded and grew and multiplied (Acts 12:24). It is not the word that Jesus spoke of as being sown by the active speaking of the ministry (Mt. 13). But *all* of these are God's *words,* as is also his speaking that we hear when we *individually hear God.*[3]

If we come to the Bible without acknowledging the living Word of God, we are in danger of treating the Bible as an end in itself. When he denounced the Pharisees, Jesus warned against our impulse to manipulate sacred Scriptures: "Woe also to you lawyers! For you load people with burdens hard to bear, and you yourselves do not lift a finger to ease them . . . you have taken away the key of knowledge; you did not enter yourselves, and you hindered those

who were entering" (Luke 11:46, 52). The Pharisees elevated obedience to the letter of the Law to an absurd level of perfectionism,
abusing it to judge and condemn others while applauding their
own self-righteousness. They concealed from people the Spirit of
the Law—the God who provided the Law. It was intended not as
a burden upon the people, but as a way of life that would enable
them to stay in relationship with their Creator, their Redeemer,
their Sustainer. This is why David could exult, "Oh, how I love
your law! It is my meditation all day long. . . . Your word is a lamp
to my feet and a light to my path" (Ps. 119:97, 105) in his extended
love letter that is the longest psalm in the Bible.

The legalism of the Pharisees is an expression of bibliolatry—a
rigid adherence to the letter of the Scriptures, devoid of the presence of the Spirit, which makes a virtual idol of the Scriptures.
Our God is not the Bible, but its living Author: "You search the
scriptures because you think that in them you have eternal life;
and it is they that testify on my behalf," said Jesus. "Yet you
refuse to come to me to have life" (John 5:39–40).

It is a short jump from bibliolatry to magic—the attempt to
manipulate the supernatural for personal benefit. A magical approach to the Bible bypasses the living God by treating the Scriptures as a sort of Ouija board, collapsing any possibility for true
relationship. Instead, the Bible becomes an oracle, overriding
human choice and responsibility—for example, when we open it
randomly and with closed eyes point a finger to wherever it lands
on the page, passively accepting the "chosen" verse as the guide
to our next decision. This is not to say that God cannot or does
not use such random means to communicate with us. God can

use any means God chooses to get our attention, but the Bible provides clear guidance for how we are to seek the Lord, and it involves the human heart, mind, and soul, not magic tricks.

The "pull" of the Scriptures upon our lives is rooted not in magic power, but in the reality of the One who speaks to us through them. The Bible is not an ordinary book with merely human authorship, for although its content has been delivered via multiple human authors, it has been divinely superintended—"all scripture is inspired by God," Paul says (2 Tim. 3:16); other translations render "God-breathed" (NIV). Peter confirms the reliability of the Scriptures by declaring, "no prophecy of scripture is a matter of one's own interpretation, because no prophecy ever came by human will, but men and women moved by the Holy Spirit spoke from God" (2 Pet. 1:20–21).

There is a life coming to us through the Bible, and we will find it as we come expectantly. The Bible invites us into life with God, but it does not try to force us into it. It leaves enough space that we can pass by this life if we desire to do so. The living Christ will not overpower us, but he does make himself available to those who want to find him. One of the primary ways he does this is through the Bible.

Our expectancy will lead us into what theologian Karl Barth calls the "strange new world within the Bible"—a grand story replete with places, people, events, cultures, and encounters that run counter to our ordinary lived experience. To enter into the life it depicts in colorful and dizzying variety—yet all pointing to the same theme of God in search of relationship with humankind—it is necessary that we come not just expectantly, but attentively.

ENTER ATTENTIVELY

Coming to the Bible attentively means, first and foremost, reading the Bible on its own terms. We can turn to Karl Barth as a guide for stepping across the threshold of everyday life into the Bible by asking with him, "What sort of house is it to which the Bible is a door? What sort of country is spread before our eyes when we throw the Bible open?"[4]

Perhaps the first reality that strikes us when we do so is *the Bible is not nice and neat.* To the unacquainted eye, it is confusing. It is not organized in clear and obvious ways. Why didn't God just give it to us straight?

Well, the straight answer to that is that the Bible is a *story.* The Bible is a collection of books with a vast array of characters and events—a vast number of stories within one really grand story. Human beings are so important to God that the divine purposes are worked out through the messiness and sprawl of human history. Apparently, it is more important to God that human beings learn his ways in freedom than it is to get things done efficiently.

Jesus was continually offending the religious professionals of his day because he broke their rules and moved outside the lines of convention. He forgave the transgressors and criticized the "obedient." You see, the condition of our hearts is more important to Jesus than how well we play by the rules. This frustrates moralists no end, because their primary concern is moral rule-keeping. It's so much easier to point the finger of blame when we can keep score on behavior. It is far more difficult to judge—and be judged by—the health of the inner life. But "the LORD does not see as mortals see; they look on the outward appearance, but the LORD looks on the heart" (1 Sam. 16:7).

If God wanted us to have the definitive Field Guide to Faith, we would have it. But then if we did have such a sacred book to answer all our questions and make everything plain, it would be easier to ignore the living God. We would not have to struggle in transforming human understanding with divine perspectives. It would be so much easier to make judgment calls and resolve arguments on difficult moral issues if somebody would simply tell us what to do.

Of course, the Bible does contain lists of dos and don'ts, but they are not the kinds of things we can easily check off a to-do list (or a don't-do list):

- "I am the LORD your God . . . you shall have no other gods before me" (Deut. 5:6–7); and "Love the LORD your God with all your heart, and with all your soul, and with all your might" (Deut. 6:5).

- "Do not be like a horse or a mule, without understanding, whose temper must be curbed with bit and bridle"; instead, submit yourself to the LORD, who will "instruct you and teach you the way you should go" (Ps. 32:8–9).

- Do not rely on religious behavior to please God or to be a moral person: "What to me is the multitude of your sacrifices? says the LORD; I have had enough of burnt offerings of rams and the fat of fed beasts. . . . Your new moons and your appointed festivals my soul hates; they have become a burden to me, I am weary of bearing them" (Isa. 1:11, 14). Instead, "cease to do evil, learn to do good; seek justice, rescue the oppressed, defend the orphan, plead for the widow" (Isa. 1:16–17).

- "Do not store up for yourselves treasures on earth . . . but store up for yourselves treasures in heaven" (Matt. 6:19–20).

- "Do nothing from selfish ambition or conceit, but in humility regard others as better than yourselves" (Phil. 2:3).

What do all the items on this list have in common? In order to fulfill them, they require relationship—relationship with God for the ability to carry them out; relationship with God and other people for the desired outcome. When Jesus was asked to sum up all the Law and the Prophets, he declared that all of them depend upon love of God and love of neighbor (Matt. 22:35–40). Jesus prized the law of love as the "so what" of all the rules of Israel's Law.

When we fail to read the Bible on its own terms, we miss its grand story—and thus the great truths to which the Bible bears witness. Some people read portions of the Old Testament and assume that what God instructed Israel to do is normative for everyone who believes in God. What a tragic miscalculation this can be, if it is used to justify armed aggression or even genocide against "unbelievers."

One of the most practical ways to read the Bible on its own terms is to read chunks of it rather than individual passages only. We read for stories, events, episodes, character profiles. When practical, we read whole books. When we come across lists of commands, such as those in Leviticus, we can read them in the context of the story of what God was doing with the people of Israel at that time. What do those rules reveal about the kind of life that God wanted them to live at that time, in that place?

When reading wisdom literature, such as the Psalms, we read them in the context of what these prayers revealed about the people's relationship to God. What, then, do they mean for our relationship with God today?

A story has elements of place (setting), plot, characters, and themes. Notice the places of the Bible—not just particular towns and nations and geographical regions, but recurring kinds of places such as mountains, valleys, and rivers. Place yourself in them imaginatively so that you begin to feel the significance of their particular characteristics. Notice objects that show up repeatedly: stones, altars, scrolls, garments, animals. Look around at the people who populate the stories—what are they like? Where do they come from? Who tends to get the lead parts? What conflicts do they face, how do they handle them, and how are they changed by going through them? Pay attention to the recurring themes of the stories of the Bible: God loves human beings; human beings always seem to want what they can't have; God is grieved and angered when human beings rebel but pursues them and forgives them anyway; God is involved not just in the lives of the chosen people, but in the lives of all peoples, and in the concerns of every living thing in creation.

When we come to the Bible attentively, we will find endless access points for how our lives can be gathered up in, and changed by, life with God. Once we begin to taste the goodness of the with-God life, we will want more of it. "The things of earth will grow strangely dim in the light of his glory and grace,"[5] and we will find ourselves hungering less for what we want, and more for what God wants.

ENTER HUMBLY

On a dusty road north of Jerusalem within a few years of the death of Jesus of Nazareth, a murderous religious zealot was literally dropped in his tracks. Armed with letters giving him the high priest's authority to search the synagogues of Damascus, the death-dealing Saul of Tarsus was intent on arresting followers of "the Way." One moment he was hot on their trail. The next moment he was flat on the ground, blinded by a great flash of light with a voice ringing in his ears: "Saul, Saul, why do you persecute me?"

"Who are you, Lord?" he asked.

"I am Jesus, whom you are persecuting. But get up and enter the city, and you will be told what you are to do."

Saul was led by the hand into Damascus. He spent the next three days in seclusion, praying and fasting and waiting, still sightless. When a disciple named Ananias came and laid hands on him, Saul's sight was restored and he received the Holy Spirit. He was baptized in the name of Jesus, and soon he was in the very synagogues he had formerly targeted for persecution. He had turned from meting out death to offering life, proclaiming that Jesus was, indeed, the Messiah. (For the biblical account of these events, see Luke's retelling in Acts 9:1–25 and Paul's own account of these events in Acts 22:1–21; Acts 26:1–23; and Gal. 1:13ff.) The world-shaking ministry of Saul, now Paul the servant of Christ, was underway.

Although Paul's conversion took place under exceptional circumstances, the event has universal significance for the ways of God with humankind:

- We find God because God comes searching for us.

- Ultimately, we are not in control of our lives—God is.

- God addresses us personally in the context of what God is doing with us corporately as the people of God.

- The manifestation of God's presence lays us out flat, figuratively if not literally. When we get up again, our direction and purpose in life are utterly transformed.

Reading the Bible for spiritual transformation is tantamount to inviting a Damascus road experience. If we venture onto the ancient roads of the Bible's world with an open mind and an inquiring heart, we can expect to encounter the living God. All we need do is ask Saul's question: "Who are you, Lord?" Scripture is filled with the promise of the Lord's reply.

A third way, then, to bring our lives into the with-God life of the Bible is by entering *humbly*. How do we do this? Well, when we sit down to read, we can start with a few minutes of prayerful silence. We can still every motion that is not rooted in the desire to experience God's presence in our reading, waiting until we sense that inwardly we are quiet, hushed, expectant.

To help offset the tendency to focus on our favorite passages, or to jump to a conclusion about what a particular passage means, I have found it helpful to read through the entire passage once, out loud. Then I go back a second time, reading silently, but this time highlighting the passages that seem particularly significant. A third time, I go back and read through only the highlighted passages to see if a particular image, phrase, or verse lifts itself to my attention. (I will often write out that excerpt on an index card and carry it with me throughout the day for reflection whenever I have the chance to read it again.)

This is one way of seeking the gentle leading of God's Spirit. Such humble submission to the text allows God to shape the attitude and posture of our hearts. There is a great freedom in such submission—the freedom to lay down the heavy burden of "getting it right," of seeing what we think we need to see. We will also find liberating relief from trying to control the Bible, to make *it* "come out right." Instead, as we read, we will find ourselves inwardly praying, *Pour the living water that flows from Christ through the Bible into my dry and thirsty soul.*

God promises that when we seek him, it will not be in vain. "[When] you call upon me and come and pray to me, I will hear you," God says through the prophet Jeremiah. "When you search for me, you will find me; if you seek me with all your heart, I will let you find me" (Jer. 29:13–14). The writer to the Hebrews declares, "[God] rewards those who seek him" (11:6).

Transformation takes place as we discover that in surrendering to how God chooses to speak through the Scriptures, we are no longer so attached to *our* concerns and *our* anxious needs. We will want to shed them as dry husks, because they wither next to the radical freshness of life offered to us through Jesus dwelling within. Our formerly self-serving and self-protecting agendas will seem small-minded next to becoming purposeful, active participants in the kingdom-of-God-with-us.

The Bible makes clear that God's primary agenda is to create an all-inclusive community of loving persons with the living God as the very center of this community as its prime Sustainer and most glorious Inhabitant (cf. Eph. 2:19–22; 3:10). What will it be

like to live in this perfect community? We have a beautiful vision
of it from the Apostle John's Revelation:

> I saw the holy city, the new Jerusalem, coming down out of
>   heaven from God, prepared as a bride adorned for her hus-
>   band. And I heard a loud voice from the throne saying,
> "See, the home of God is among mortals.
> He will dwell with them;
> they will be his peoples,
> and God himself will be with them;
> he will wipe every tear from their eyes.
> Death will be no more;
> mourning and crying and pain will be no more,
> for the first things have passed away." (Rev. 21:2–4)

When we read humbly, in a constant attitude of repentance—
that is, turning away from our own perspective to seek God's
perspective—we will begin to grasp the spiritual riches that God
has made available to all humanity in the written Word.

One of the most poignant images in the Bible is of Jesus,
stripped down to a towel wrapped around his waist, a basin of
water in hand, preparing to wash the feet of his incredulous disciples. The Gospel of John records that at this point, Jesus knew
the agony of his death was imminent. In his last evening on
earth, he chose to spend it humbly, loving his disciples well.
Knowing that "he had come from God and was going to God"
enabled him to surrender his life in sacrificial service to his Abba
and to those whom he had been sent in love (John 13:3).

The Bible is the means through which we are introduced to Jesus and invited to follow him in this life of humility and service. Secured by the knowledge that in Christ, our origin is God and our destination is God, we will yield the fruit of service to others. This is the "so what" of our Bible reading. Does it shape our spirits in love and humility? Does it lead us more fully into life with God?

When we come to the Bible expectantly, attentively, and humbly, we will experience the joy of losing ourselves in the great river of Life that is life, indeed. That is what the Bible is all about: human life eternally bound up in divine Life. Even now God is writing us into the beautiful culmination of this grand story: human beings as the dwelling place of God who is fully present with them. This is the dynamic of the great *Immanuel Principle*—the "God with us" way of life.

3

Experiencing the with-God Life

My dwelling place shall be with them; and I will be their God, and they shall be my people.
—Ezek. 37:27

Throughout all of human history, the voice of God resounds with absolute assurance: "I am with you." This news does not come to us as some intellectual proposition we must accept at face value. It is not bound up in academic doctrine packaged for religious scholars, nor in arcane rumors of supernatural activity in celestial arenas. Rather, it is a reality that unfolds before us in breathtaking detail, mediated through the actual experience of individuals, families, tribes, cities, nations, and generations. Over and over, God said:

- to Isaac at Beersheba, on the move in search of a new home far away from the Philistines: "Do not be afraid, for I am with you and will bless you" (Gen. 26:24).

- to Jacob at Bethel, escaping from the murderous fury of his brother, Esau: "I am with you and will keep you wherever you go" (Gen. 28:15).

- to Joshua, crossing the Jordan, leading the people in the conquest of the Promised Land: "I will be with you as I was with Moses" (Josh. 3:7).

- to David, newly installed as king through the prophet Nathan: "Do all that you have in mind, for God is with you" (1 Chron. 17:2).

- through the prophet Isaiah, to the people of Israel under threat from the Babylonians: "Do not fear, for I am with you, do not be afraid, for I am your God; I will strengthen you, I will help you, I will uphold you with my victorious right hand" (Isa. 41:9–10).

- to the prophet Jeremiah, called to a ministry that would make his life miserable and under constant threat: "Do not be afraid of them, for I am with you to deliver you, says the LORD" (Jer. 1:7–8).

- through Jeremiah, to the people of the divided kingdom who would soon be scattered into exile in judgment upon their disobedience: ". . . do not be dismayed, O Israel; for I am going to save you from far away, and your offspring from the land of their captivity. Jacob shall return and have quiet and ease, and no one shall make him afraid. For I am with you, says the LORD, to save you. . ." (Jer. 30:10–11).

- through the prophet Zephaniah, bearing news of judgment and hope to the people of the divided kingdom nearing the end of a corrupt era of material comfort and rampant immorality: "The LORD your God is with you, he is mighty to save. He will take great delight in you, he will quiet you with his love, he will rejoice over you with singing" (Zeph. 3:17, NIV).

- through the prophet Haggai, to the returning exiles called to rebuild the temple amid the temptation to complacency and self-concern: "I am with you" (Hag. 1:13).

- through the risen Christ, to the disciples as they were commissioned to carry forth his work into all the world: "And remember, I am with you always, to the end of the age" (Matt. 28:20).

- to the Apostle Paul in Corinth, under threat from the Jews as well as the Romans: "Do not be afraid, but speak and do not be silent; for I am with you, and no one will lay a hand on you to harm you, for there are many in this city who are my people" (Acts 18:9–10).

- to all those in the new heaven and new earth, as the glorious city, the New Jerusalem, materializes before them: "See, the home of God is among mortals. He will dwell with them; they will be his peoples, and God himself will be with them; he will wipe every tear from their eyes. Death will be no more; mourning and crying and pain will be no more, for the first things have passed away" (Rev. 21:3–4).

The Bible does not simply tell us of the presence of God; it shows us the active presence of God deeply and permanently embedded in all the smells, tastes, touches, sights, and sounds of human life. Over and over, this reality is played out in stories, poems, carefully preserved histories, records of cultural systems, details of prophetic revelations, speeches, letters, songs, and prayers. The Scripture weaves the involvement of God through the intimacies of birth and death, lovemaking and betrayal, weddings and funerals, labor and rest, warring and peacemaking, wealth and poverty, hunger and thirst, tears and laughter. Across thousands of years, with wave upon wave of names and faces and recurring events, the Bible threads God's patient words of love and faithfulness: *I am with you.*

THE FREEDOM TO CHOOSE

The Bible reveals God to us as both Initiator and Pursuer. The beauty of the primeval Garden shows us a Creator who summoned a vast universe into existence and capped this astonishing feat by breathing the *imago dei* into its clay so that Creator and creature could enjoy the mutual awareness of intimate relationship. This special creature was not simply another living being, but a *person* placed in the Garden as a fellow caretaker with the God of this beautiful home. Human beings could work and rest and enjoy intimate partnership in the unforced rhythms of life as it was meant to be—life in communion with their Creator, with one another, and with all living things.

In the twenty-first century, thanks to the science of sophisticated instruments such as the *Voyager 1* spacecraft—now reaching the edge of our solar system after traversing nearly nine billion miles—we are glimpsing a universe so vast that we can barely touch the edge of its garment with our understanding. Millennia ago, with only the barest of human lenses, our predecessors could see far enough into the night sky to know they were dwarfed by the immensity of the world around them. All the more reason, then, to marvel that the God of such a creation would be so intimately involved with human beings:

> When I look at your heavens, the work of your fingers,
> the moon and the stars that you have established;
> what are human beings that you are mindful of them,
> mortals that you care for them?
> Yet you have made them a little lower than God,
> and crowned them with glory and honor. (Ps. 8:3–5)

And yet the psalmist makes it clear that human beings have a relationship with God that is set apart from that of all creation:

> You have given them dominion over the works of your
>   hands;
> you have put all things under their feet,
> all sheep and oxen,
> and also the beasts of the field,
> the birds of the air, and the fish of the sea,
> whatever passes along the paths of the seas. (Ps. 8:6–8)

Today we see the beginning of a collective concern across the globe for how carelessly we have exercised such dominion. Yet

even as we attempt to calculate the damaging cost of our consumption upon the number of whales in the ocean or salmon in
our rivers or old-growth forests in our wildernesses, we are
drawn again to marvel at the teeming life in the waters and the
hidden worlds stair-stepped from forest floors to treetops. For
such as these, we were brought into the world. Through them,
we hear the voice of our Creator: *I am with you.*

For the abundant life that surges around us and through us,
for the knowledge that God has created all of it so that we might
enjoy divine companionship and partnership through it, we can
only burst into praise: "O Lord, our Sovereign, how majestic is
your name in all the earth!" (Ps. 8:1).

But we are also well acquainted with the psalmist's lament,
"Why, O Lord, do you stand far off? Why do you hide yourself in
times of trouble?" (Ps. 10:1). When evil runs rampant, when the
earth convulses in earthquakes and tidal waves, when loved ones
are torn from us, we are seized with fear that God is absent or no
longer in control. We know what it is like to be separated from
God. Here is the very first picture of it: "They heard the sound of
the Lord God walking in the garden at the time of the evening
breeze, and the man and his wife hid themselves from the presence of the Lord God among the trees of the garden" (Gen. 3:8).

From the outset, God has made clear to us that we have the
freedom to choose for or against the with-God life. Obedience is
mandated for our well-being but not imposed by force. Planted
in the midst of Eden's abundance was something withheld from
us. If we reached for it, God warned, it would destroy us. Im-
printed in our genetic code was the ancient knowledge that obedience means life; disobedience means death.

When our ancestors chose the one thing forbidden to them, their act tore open a deep split in the center of the world. The creation itself was subjected to "futility," to "bondage to decay" (Rom. 8:20–21). The human heart was divided and became at war with itself: "I can will what is right, but I cannot do it. For I do not do the good I want, but the evil I do not want is what I do" (Rom. 7:18–19). Adam and Eve tasted the bitter fruits of independence: with their Creator, shame and fear instead of intimacy and trust; with one another, betrayal and manipulation undermining respect and kindness; with the beautiful world around them, exile and struggle instead of home and harmony. For all of us, this deep split means that desire for God is laced through with the rebellious impulse to reject God.

However, in the Bible's plotline, sooner or later bad news is always followed by good news. God allowed Adam and Eve to suffer the consequences of their choice, but God did not abandon them. In fact, God came after them while they were hiding in shame. Although our choice to turn away from God strips us of the felt assurance of God's presence, it does not have the power to expel us from God's presence. God has created a sacred space of human freedom in which our transformation can take place.

Our loss of unknowing innocence means that we must develop the kind of character and identity that will freely seek harmony with God. If we continue to choose life apart from God, we will take on an identity that focuses exclusively on ourselves, and we will then try to master our life and our world on our own—just what happened in the Garden, leading to the dreadful decline catalogued in Paul's letter to the Romans: "For though they knew God, they did not honor him as God or give thanks to him, but they became futile in their thinking, and their senseless minds were darkened" (1:21). The natural consequences of disobedience led to an earth "filled with violence," where "every inclination of the thoughts of their hearts was only evil continually" (Gen. 6:11, 5).

But God chooses to be with us in spite of our flight. God the Initiator becomes God the Pursuer—not to destroy us for our disobedience, but to turn us away from it and draw us back to life. The Apostle Paul explains, "But God proves his love for us in that while we still were sinners Christ died for us" (Rom. 5:8). Through God's sustaining presence in Christ, the Unifier of all things on heaven and on earth (see Eph. 1:10; Col. 1:20), the consequences of our disobedience do not have to lead to eternal separation from God. We can choose the freedom of life in Christ: "There is therefore now no condemnation for those who are in Christ Jesus. For the law of the Spirit of life in Christ Jesus has set you free from the law of sin and of death" (Rom. 8:1–2).

You see, this life in God does not depend on our own efforts. It is a free gift: "For by grace you have been saved through faith, and this is not your own doing; it is the gift of God—not the result of works, so that no one may boast" (Eph. 2:8–9). Will we choose this gift—here, now, in this present moment of our life?

THE POWER TO CHANGE

The divine assurance thundering throughout the ages is also a divine invitation:

"I am with you—will you be with Me?"

This dynamic is the absolute unifying center of the Bible. Every story in the Bible, no matter its twists and turns, whether the human characters are trustworthy or untrustworthy, whether the story is sad or happy, is built on this clarion call to relationship. "I am with you—will you be with Me?"

"Incline your ear, and come to me; listen, so that you may live," God calls to us through the prophet Isaiah (55:3). When we lose our way through disobedience, we must learn how to turn back toward God. From Genesis to Revelation, throughout human history, the Bible tells the stories of people learning to turn back to God. Always, it is God's grace and power drawing them and supporting them, giving them the means to become transformed into the kind of people who will gladly and freely choose life in the eternally loving community of God's People. God wants relationship with us, not mechanical transactions. And so he teaches us through the flesh and blood of ordinary people whose wayward steps were straightened and made firm by the power of God at work among them.

As we read and reread the Bible's stories, we learn how life with God takes place in the rough and tumble of real-life situations. The crucible of change is our everyday world. The tools of our transformation are the choices arising from our everyday circumstances. The Bible fleshes out this with-God life in the give-and-take of everyday experiences. If we will allow them, these stories can draw us in irresistibly until they become emblematic of our story, as well.

We read of Abraham trudging up Mount Moriah, struggling with the decision to sacrifice Isaac, and we hear God speaking to us, too. The *Kol Yahweh,* the voice of the Lord, is calling us to surrender our most priceless possession—and in that surrender, the meaning of "my" and "mine" are changed forever.

We follow the Israelites from their exciting Exodus from Egypt into the boredom, uncertainty, and fear of wandering in the wilderness. In their wandering, we see our own travel across unknown landscapes, and we learn to focus on God instead of on how soon we will make it to the next place of safety and whether we will have bread or meat for tomorrow.

We meditate on the angelic encounter with Mary, and we feel the combination of fear and joy in the direct call of God. We, too, are invited to respond to the divine call with the overwhelming word of obedience: "Behold, I am a servant of the Lord; let it be to me according to your word" (Luke 1:38).

We see Peter walking on water, and we, too, are challenged to take up the humanly impossible task in our contemporary world, possible only if we will fix our gaze on Jesus and not look away in fear.

We watch Moses standing dumb before the burning bush, and we, too, must be reminded to take off our shoes when God reveals to us that where we are standing is holy ground. We learn that wherever we are—in our homes, in our work, with neighbors and friends—God is present with us, at work to transform us into people who will carry on the liberating work of the kingdom of God.

We read the story of Jonah, and we understand how resistance to God's ways manifests itself in nationalism and racism. Then we recognize the same spirit of rebellion and disobedience in ourselves, as well. As we turn in repentance, we are transformed yet another time into people who are more likely to love than hate, to unify rather than divide.

We are drawn into the story of David acting on his lust for Bathsheba, and we recognize that the spirit of lust and possessiveness has taken up residence in us, too. We understand that our bodies themselves are testing places for our character, not mere vehicles of gratification.

We marvel at the courage of Esther and long that we, too, might have the same holy courage for the tough decisions of life. We realize that all the little choices we make in each ordinary day of our lives shape us in ways that prepare us—or not—for the big choices that can face us unexpectedly in an instant.

We learn from Daniel's confidence in the lions' den, a confidence born out of an unshakable belief in a living God, and we, too, long to believe in a living God. We learn that "faith is the assurance of things hoped for, the conviction of things not seen," and that Daniel's story of faith has been preserved and retold—along with all the other stories recounted in the Scriptures—for our benefit, surrounding us with a "great cloud of witnesses" for encouragement in our journey of faith (Heb. 11:1; 12:1).

And we learn most of all from Jesus, "the pioneer and perfecter of our faith, who for the sake of the joy that was set before him endured the cross, disregarding its shame, and has taken his seat at the right hand of the throne of God" (Heb. 12:23).

TRUSTING, SIMPLY TRUSTING

With extraordinary patience, God gathered a people from all the peoples of the earth through whom he could demonstrate his love and faithfulness for the whole world. But as the history of

God's people shows, human beings are not always reliable part-
ners in the Divine-human adventure. Under the old covenant of
Law, God made a unilateral commitment to his people. Their
faithlessness could not break God's covenant of faithfulness.
Through all of Israel's experiences—from slavery and oppression, to conquest and growth, to the height of its kingdom and
then back into exile—God used their circumstances to strengthen
them in obedience and chasten them in disobedience, restoring
relationship when it was broken. All of this was done to prepare
the way for the coming Messiah who would establish a new covenant of grace, fulfilling "what had been spoken by the LORD
through the prophet: 'Look, the virgin shall conceive and bear a
son, and they shall name him Emmanuel,' which means, 'God is
with us'" (Matt. 1:23, cf. Isa. 7:14).

In Jesus Christ, God himself fulfilled "a new covenant with
the house of Israel and with the house of Judah; not like the covenant that I made with their ancestors. . . . This is the covenant
that I will make with the house of Israel . . . I will put my laws in
their minds, and write them on their hearts, and I will be their
God, and they shall be my people" (Heb. 8:8–10). Thus God
became not only the Initiator, not just the Pursuer, but also the
Guarantor of relationship.

God has set eternity in our hearts (see Eccles. 3:11, NIV). We
are restless until we find our rest in God. And, indeed, life with
God is a form of rest—not the absence of effort, but the absence
of *self*-effort: "His divine power has given us everything needed
for life and godliness, through the knowledge of him who called
us by his own glory and goodness" (2 Pet. 1:3).

How, then, do we step into the richness and power of this life?

That is, in essence, the question asked by the disciples, troubled by Jesus' talk of his coming departure. Jesus had assured them of his presence with them: "Do not let your hearts be troubled. Believe in God, believe also in me. In my Father's house there are many dwelling places. If it were not so, would I have told you that I go to prepare a place for you? And if I go and prepare a place for you, I will come again and will take you to myself, so that where I am, there you may be also. And you know the way to the place where I am going." But Thomas objected, "Lord, we do not know where you are going. How can we know the way?"

Jesus answered, "I am the way, and the truth, and the life. No one comes to the Father except through me. If you know me, you will know my Father also. From now on you do know him and have seen him" (John 14:1–7).

Here is the central mystery of life with God: *the way into it is simply by trusting in Jesus.* "Do not fear, only believe," he said to Jairus, whose daughter was dying (Mark 5:36). To the crowds who had followed him to Capernaum, asking what they had to do in order to perform righteous works, Jesus responded, "This is the work of God, that you believe in him whom he has sent" (John 6:28–29). To Nicodemus, struggling to understand what Jesus meant by entering the kingdom through being "born from above," Jesus proclaimed, "For God so loved the world that he gave his only Son, so that everyone who believes in him may not perish but may have eternal life" (John 3:16).

Jesus proclaimed the good news to people who were used to endless rules and hard-to-keep requirements as the means of acceptance by God. The simplicity of his message was so stunning that for some, it was impossible to accept.

Today, we struggle to analyze and dissect this simple command to "believe," trying to wrap our minds around something we will never fully understand. That is because trusting in Jesus is ultimately not a matter of the mind, but of the heart. Jesus used a variety of word pictures to describe himself in relation to us, and all of them have emotional power to stir the heart. We want to pin down the nature of belief, reduce it to a series of propositions to which we can sign our names, use it as a way to control who is in and who is out. But trusting Jesus is not a matter of assenting to various propositions; it is an act of relationship.

The Gospel of John records the great "I Am" statements of Jesus, in which he declares himself to us, inviting us into life in the kingdom he came proclaiming. In the following statements, listen to the ways in which Jesus describes himself. Read each passage slowly, and reflect on what it implies about relationship:

- "I am the bread of life. Whoever comes to me will never be hungry, and whoever believes in me will never be thirsty" (John 6:35).

- "Let anyone who is thirsty come to me, and let the one who believes in me drink. As the scripture has said, 'Out of the believer's heart shall flow rivers of living water'" (John 7:37–38).

- "I am the light of the world. Whoever follows me will never walk in darkness but will have the light of life" (John 8:12).

- "I am the good shepherd. The good shepherd lays down his life for the sheep" (John 10:11).

- "I am the gate for the sheep. . . . Whoever enters by me will be saved, and will come in and go out and find pasture. The thief comes only to steal and kill and destroy. I came that they may have life, and have it abundantly" (John 10:7, 9–10).

- "I am the way, and the truth, and the life. . . . If you continue in my word, you are truly my disciples; and you will know the truth, and the truth will make you free" (John 14:6; 8:31–32).

- "I am the resurrection and the life. Those who believe in me, even though they die, will live, and everyone who lives and believes in me will never die" (John 11:25).

- "I am the true vine, and my Father is the vinegrower. . . . Abide in me as I abide in you. . . . I am the vine, you are the branches. Those who abide in me and I in them bear much fruit, because apart from me you can do nothing" (John 15:1, 4, 5).

- And then we also have the imagery in John's Gospel of the name given to Jesus by John the Baptist, foretold by Isaiah and later to figure so prominently in the Apostle John's Revelation: "Here is the Lamb of God who takes away the sin of the world!" (John 1:29).

These are images to feed on for a lifetime. We know that our character is shaped by what we immerse ourselves in. Immerse yourself in these wondrous images of Christ, and they will feed your faith, strengthening your desire to trust Jesus for everything.

Have you ever felt that you simply did not have the ability to trust? Consider the story of the anguished father who brought his boy, tormented by an "unclean spirit," to Jesus after the disciples were unable to heal him. "If you are able to do anything, have pity on us and help us," he pleaded with Jesus.

Jesus responded by calling him into trust in God's unlimited power: "If you are able!—All things can be done for the one who believes."

To this the man responded with one of the most honest cries in all of Scripture: "I believe; help my unbelief!" (see Mark 9:14–29). Belief is not something we have to work up to on our own. It is not a special talent that some people are born with and others are not. Ultimately, belief in Jesus is a resting of the heart that is prompted by the Spirit and undergirded by the Spirit. That is why Paul assured the Romans, "When we cry 'Abba! Father!' it is that very Spirit bearing witness with our spirit that we are children of God" (Rom. 8:15–16). It is why he explained to those suffering in Corinth, "But it is God who establishes us with you in Christ and has anointed us, by putting his seal on us and giving us his Spirit in our hearts as a first installment" (2 Cor. 1:21–22).

The ability to respond to God's call in Christ does not rest with us, but is wholly the work of God. It cannot be forced on anyone, nor can we force it on ourselves in order to please others. Jesus gives us supernatural ability to trust in him—but if we cut ourselves off from relationship with him, we also cut ourselves off from the means of developing this ability.

CHOOSING TO TRUST

This is why the supreme act of spiritual formation is allowing our all-sufficient Savior to perfect his will and way in our lives. God is involved with each one of us, patiently at work to lead us in gradual and humble steps through all the twists and turns and successes and failures of our lives. As we exercise our freedom by choosing to trust in Christ, we discover the depths of life with God. We become shaped in the image of the One with whom we spend time and to whom we give our hearts.

In his letter to the Colossians, the Apostle Paul takes on the false teaching that growth in Christian faith can be achieved by special knowledge or practices. "See to it that no one takes you captive through philosophy and empty deceit, according to human tradition . . . and not according to Christ. For in him the whole fullness of deity dwells bodily, and you have come to fullness in him, who is the head of every ruler and authority" (2:8–10). His teaching about Christ in this epistle provides some of the most soaring testimony in all of Scripture to the mystery and beauty of life with God: "So if you have been raised with Christ, seek the things that are above, where Christ is, seated at the right hand of God. Set your minds on things that are above, not on things that are on earth, for you have died, and your life is hidden with Christ in God. When Christ who is your life is revealed, then you also will be revealed with him in glory" (3:1–4).

God is with you. The Bible reveals "the mystery that has been hidden throughout the ages and generations but has now been revealed to his saints. To them God chose to make known how great among the Gentiles are the riches of the glory of this mystery, which is Christ in you, the hope of glory" (Col. 1:26–27). God has given you the freedom to choose, the power to change, and the ability to trust. *God is with you.* Will you choose to be with God?

Part 2

Nurturing the Intention

It was this . . . intention that made the primitive Christians such eminent instances of piety, that made the goodly fellowship of the Saints and all the glorious army of martyrs and confessors. And if you will here stop and ask yourself why you are not as pious as the primitive Christians were, your own heart will tell you that it is neither through ignorance nor inability, but purely because you never thoroughly intended it.

—William Law,
*A Serious Call to a Devout
and Holy Life*

4
_____

Reading with the Heart

I pray that the God of our Lord Jesus Christ, the Father of
glory, may give you a spirit of wisdom and revelation as
you come to know him, so that, with the eyes of your heart
enlightened, you may know what is the hope to which he
has called you.

—Ephesians 1:17–18

There is a vast difference between reading the surface of the biblical text and encountering the God who divinely superintended
its delivery into our hands—the God who proclaims to you and
to me, "I am *with* you ... will you be *with* Me?" A story in the
Gospel of John offers a marvelous way to depict the difference
between these two approaches to Scripture.

The narrative places us just outside Jerusalem's city walls
"early on the first day of the week, while it was still dark," with
Mary Magdalene at the tomb where Jesus was buried (see John
20:1–18). Shocked to see the boulder pushed aside from the
tomb's entrance and the body missing, Mary rushes to alert
Peter and John. All three run back to the tomb together. After
examining the contents of the tomb—neatly folded death cloths

punctuating the body's disappearance—the male disciples "believe" and return home. Still agonizing, Mary stays behind.

We don't know why these early witnesses responded so differently to what they saw—was it a gender issue? Peter and John had new information, and they acted on it. Mary, longing for encounter, remained distraught. When two angels appear and ask why she is weeping, Mary does not recognize them as supernatural visitors, even though the text suggests their clothing was unusual. Through her curtain of tears, Mary simply repeats the same stunning news she had given Peter and John: "They have taken the Lord out of the tomb, and we do not know where they have laid him."

Mary turns around and sees a man standing nearby, mistaking him for the gardener. "Why are you weeping, and whom are you looking for?" he asks. She begs him to tell her if he had moved the body. Her heartbreak turns to joyful astonishment when the risen Christ reveals himself to her with one word: *"Mary."*

The Gospel account does not indicate why Mary didn't immediately recognize Jesus. In several of Jesus' post-resurrection visits, the disciples he visits appear to have been prevented from identifying him until a particular moment of revelation—a miraculous catch of fish after a long, fruitless night when a "stranger" tells them to lower their nets once more; a mealtime moment when a "stranger" takes bread in his hands and breaks it . . . and the moment when a "stranger" speaks Mary's name.

Reading Scripture with human "eyes" alone is like mentally registering the words of the text without recognizing who is speaking through them. This is why Paul speaks of "the eyes of your heart" through which we acquire experiential knowledge of God

(Eph. 1:17–18). Jesus promises that the Father will send in his name the Holy Spirit, our "Advocate," who would guide us into all truth (John 14:26). Just as Mary recognizes Jesus when he spoke her name, so we can expect to recognize the voice of God speaking personally to us in the inner sanctuary of our waiting hearts.

ALLOWING THE SPIRIT TO GUIDE US

The simplest place to start in reading with the heart is by inviting the Spirit of Christ to be our guide. Whether we sit down to read just a few verses, a psalm, or an entire book of the Bible, we prepare the eyes of our heart by praying with the hymn writer:

O send Thy Spirit, Lord, now unto me,
That He may touch my eyes and make me see;
Show me the truth concealed within Thy word,
For in Thy book revealed I see Thee, Lord.[6]

It may sound easy to "allow the Spirit to guide us" while reading the Bible—and, indeed, it is neither difficult nor burdensome—but in a culture of consumerized Christianity it is also easy to stumble over preconceived notions about the Bible cluttering the path.

Chief among such market-driven notions is that the Bible exists to serve our needs. It is no surprise that in a consumer-driven culture we would be tempted to reduce the Bible to a product for self-improvement. But to do so is deadly.

Seeking reassurance that our lives will be safe and comfortable, we pull verses out of context and create Bible promise books listed piecemeal and arranged thematically by need. It is not wrong to hope for safety and for comfort, but that is not where we will find meaning for our lives.

In our desire for a packaged, user-friendly, "just tell me what to do" life of faith, we distort the Bible into an owners' manual for successful living. Or even moral living: then we can judge ourselves superior to others if we follow the rules more faithfully than they. It is not wrong to strive for a moral life, but if that is our only goal, it will steer us toward the righteousness of the Pharisees and not into the fullness of life with God. There is a reason why Paul counseled the Philippians, "work out your own salvation with fear and trembling" (2:12). God is concerned with the process of our growth, not in our human estimation of how well we accomplish it. Moralism flattens life with God by draining off the dimension of relationship. After all, it is much easier to follow a to-do list than to engage in the messy business of personal relations. Again, God is saying, "I am with you—will you be with Me?"

We misconstrue reading and studying the Bible as acts of self-improvement by using them as props to make us feel good about ourselves as religiously devout. You see, we can feel better about ourselves if we can point to things we are "doing for God."

All these Bible-related activities may give us some temporary satisfaction, the way eating sweets may fleetingly gratify a sweet tooth. But just as a pastry is no substitute for solid life-giving food, so using the Bible to serve our needs will leave untouched the deepest longings of our soul. Staying immersed in the Bible can keep us on course on our spiritual path. However, it is entirely possible for us to immerse ourselves in regular routines of spiritual practice without ever becoming more loving people.

The difference lies in our willingness to relinquish all attempts to control and manipulate the written word through submission to the transforming activity of the living Word. As Paul counseled Timothy:

Continue in what you have learned and firmly believed, knowing from whom you learned it, and how from childhood you have known the sacred writings that are able to instruct you for salvation through faith in Christ Jesus. All scripture is inspired by God and is useful for teaching, for reproof, for correction, and for training in righteousness, so that everyone who belongs to God may be proficient, equipped for every good work. (2 Tim. 3:14–17)

In a culture that places such a high premium on accomplishment, it is tempting for us to amass biblical skills in order to impress others with the knowledge and insight we presume to have gained through reading, studying, or memorizing the Bible. But the Bible itself undercuts such posturing. One of the central themes in the story of God's people is the stubbornness with which they cling to religious performance instead of clinging to God. In the second chapter of his thundering letter to the Romans, Paul goes straight for the jugular of religious hypocrisy—"[you] boast of your relation to God and know his will and determine what is best because you are instructed in the law." Religiosity corrodes the soul and bars the door to faith: "The name of God is blasphemed among the Gentiles because of you" (2:17–18, 24). We exploit the Bible to call down judgment on others instead of allowing the Bible to judge the content of our own hearts. God is in relentless pursuit of the content of our hearts: "a person is a Jew who is one inwardly, and real circumcision is a matter of the heart—it is spiritual and not literal. Such a person receives praise not from others but from God" (2:29).

The Bible is not a tool for sharpening our religious competence, but a living and active sword for cleaving our double-minded thoughts and motives, exposing and transforming the contents of our hearts (see Heb. 4:12). The best guard against any handling of the Scripture that leaves our souls untouched—and ourselves unchanged—is surrender to the cleansing, forming flow of the Holy Spirit. Simply, this means opening our whole selves—mind, body, spirit; thoughts, behavior, will—to the open page before us. We seek far more than familiarity with the text alone; instead we are focusing our attention through and beyond the text to the God whose reality fills its depths.

EXPERIENCING *LECTIO DIVINA*

Distinct from other ways of approaching the Bible, the ancient Christian practice of *lectio divina* (spiritual reading) is the primary mode of reading the Bible for transformation. There is a place for reading large portions of the Bible in one sitting, such as an entire book, but this is not it. Here we are concerned with depth rather than breadth. There is also a place for Bible study, in which we apply exegetical tools of interpretation, but this is not "study" per se. Rather, lectio is a way of allowing the mind to "descend" into the heart, so that both mind and heart might be drawn into the love and goodness of God. Our goal is immersion. We are shaped by the environment in which we live and breathe and interact.

Lectio immerses us in the deep and timeless waters of God, that more of God's eternal life might flow into our time-bound lives.

In its classic form, lectio comprises four elements, although there are many variations on them with different wording and emphasis: *lectio* (reading with a listening spirit), *meditatio* (reflecting on what we are "hearing"), *oratio* (praying in response to this hearing), and *contemplatio* (contemplating what we will carry forward into our lives). For our purposes here, we will refer to these basic elements of lectio as *listening, reflecting, praying,* and *obeying*. When these elements are combined—regardless of sequence, for they overlap and intermingle in a circular rather than a linear way—they lead the human spirit into a dynamic interaction with the Holy Spirit.

Although lectio is central to the practice of spiritual retreat, it is by no means limited to those special times and places. You can avail yourself of this practice amid your ordinary routines, whenever you take time out to refresh your soul with a dip in the waters of God's life.

First, choose a text of Scripture, preferably a short passage or story—long enough to let your thoughts spread out but short enough to cover thoroughly in the amount of time you have. You might identify this selected text from an assignment in a Bible-reading plan or church lectionary,[7] a sermon text from a worship service, a Bible story or character you feel drawn toward, or a passage suggested to you by a spiritual mentor or in a devotional book you are currently reading. In addition to your Bible, be sure to have a pen or pencil and paper alongside.

Next, find a quiet place where you can read undisturbed. If you do not already have places of solitude built into your routines, and neither your home nor work space is conducive, be creative—park your car in a corner of an empty lot; pull off at a scenic overlook; find a small table in a coffee shop. Turn off your phone, close your daily planner, put anything distracting out of eyesight, and place yourself physically and mentally in a posture of listening, of receiving. Still yourself within by breathing deeply, quieting the clamor of demands and distractions. Do not rush this part. Inward stillness is as important to spiritual reading as muscle-stretching is to a workout. Even the busiest among us can bracket our reading in this way. You might be surprised how long a mere sixty seconds of silent, prayerful breathing can feel when it wheels to a halt the grinding momentum of a hectic day. Consider how many times throughout the day you fritter away a minute on something inconsequential, with nothing to show for it. Then notice how you feel after sixty seconds of stilling your soul before God. Once you taste it, you will find yourself longing for it more and more.

As you ease into silence, allow the Holy Spirit to ease your spirit into a repose of divine expectancy, hushed and ready to listen. Breathe a quiet prayer of preparation, with or without words. Now you are ready to cross the threshold of "ordinary" life into pure and concentrated life with God.

Listening

Henri Nouwen once directed my attention to a lovely picture hanging in his apartment and said simply, "That is *lectio divina*." The painting depicted a woman with an open Bible in her lap, but her gaze was lifted upward. You understand, I am sure. We are coming to the text and seeing through the text, even beyond the text, to the Lord of the text.

We may begin by reading the passage all the way through without pausing. We are simply taking in what we read in an attitude of expectancy, as the woman in Nouwen's picture, fixing our gaze upward. All the while, we are listening for the heart of the Holy Spirit beating within our own hearts. Reading with the eyes of the heart.

After an initial reading, it is helpful to read again, slowly, this time pausing to highlight or underline any word or phrase that seems to lift itself to our attention. We have no need to struggle, trying to second-guess what God wants to teach us. We do not have to be anxious, wondering if God will bring anything or nothing to our attention. This is a time to lean into the Holy Spirit, trusting in God, wonderfully cut loose from our own internal agendas, glad in the knowledge that "the Lord is near to all who call on him" (Ps. 145:18). Through the text of Scripture, God is saying, "I am with you—will you be with Me?"

Reflecting

We come to the Scriptures predisposed to understanding them based upon our surface contexts of familiarity. This is why it is so important to breathe a prayer for the Spirit's immersing of our mind and heart into the Life of God in our reading. God can speak to us through a passage we previously overlooked, or through a familiar passage in a way we have never seen before, because our ears are prepared to hear it in a new and deeper way.

After listening, we quietly turn to reflecting, going back over the portions of the text we marked as significant, this time seeking just a single phrase or insight that is God's word to us in this time. For example, suppose we are reflecting on the risen Christ's appearance to Mary, and we have been drawn to the one word that changes her ability to see Jesus: the sound of him speaking her name. Our concern is not with the theological implications of this appearance, nor with the physics of Christ's resurrection body, nor with the meaning for the Church that Jesus broke cultural conventions in making his first appearance to a woman rather than to a man. Rather, our goal is imaginatively to take Mary's place. Ignatius of Loyola encourages us to apply all our senses to the task: Is the sky beginning to lighten? Is the air cool to the touch, and fragrant with the aroma of plants and flowers? Are the tears drying yet on our cheeks? What does "the stranger" look like before we recognize him? How do we feel physically when we hear the sound of his voice? What does our own name sound like on his lips? How would we describe the feelings now surging through us as we realize it is Jesus?

As our minds are working through such details, our spirits are alert to what, if any, connections the Spirit may be revealing between this passage and the particulars of our own lives. Inwardly we are asking, *How are you revealing yourself to me, Lord? What am I to see and understand in this border territory where my life merges with yours?* Listening in this way requires only our attention and our desire.

Swimmers know the sensation of slipping completely underwater and feeling their ears fill up as noises above the water become muffled and distant, while the sense of hearing takes on an unnatural clarity and immediacy. Sound travels through water four times as quickly as through the air, but the human ear is no longer able to detect where the sounds are coming from. The outer ear can identify direction only in air, so in water the only way sound is conducted is to the inner ear through the bones of the skull, which makes it seem as if the sound originates inside our own head. In the ocean, we could be startled by the clicks of dolphins who sound as if they have swum up alongside us when in actuality they are too far away for us to see. Our hearing is configured to make sense of the sounds based upon another context entirely.

During reflection and meditation, we are floating on the depths of God, held safely in the waters of his loving presence. This is the moment in lectio when "deep calls to deep" (Ps. 42:7). Like the joyful awareness of a loved one whispering softly into our ears, we become aware of the intimately personal voice of God. We cannot pinpoint where it is coming from because suddenly it is *within* us, sounding with a heightened clarity and immediacy, reverberating in the chambers of our heart. We know without a doubt who is speaking to us. Jesus is the Good Shepherd, and his sheep know his voice.

Lectio is a powerful answer to the psalmist's lonely cry, "My soul thirsts for God, for the living God. When shall I come and behold the face of God?" (Ps. 42:2). This is the deep connection we long for but rarely receive in a Christianized subculture where, too often, talking about experiencing God substitutes for actual experience of God.

Meditating on what we hear is like taking the first bite of a tantalizing food we have been looking forward to all day. We

chew slowly, savoring its taste and texture. We swallow grate-
fully, aware of how it makes its way down to sit comfortably in
our stomach, quieting the pangs of hunger with the assurance
that our need is being met. We repeat this over and over, allowing this word or phrase to sink down into us as it spreads
throughout blood and muscle into the bones, imprinting itself
upon us in a powerful and transforming way.

Praying

Reflection so fills us that we naturally spill over into communion
with God. We want to turn to the Lover who is whispering in
our ear and look in the divine face, trace with our fingertips the
beloved features while speaking softly in return, and rejoice to
see ourselves reflected in Jesus' gaze and feel our very existence
affirmed by his intimate awareness of us. We long to exclaim
with Mary, *Rabboni!*

We are now moving into a third element of lectio—prayer.
We engage with what we are hearing by *praying* this text of
Scripture, letting the reality of this holy moment with God give
rise to our heart cry of gratitude, confession, lament, relief, or
praise. As we complete the circle of listening and speaking, we
know that this written word of God to all people has become the
living word of God to us personally. Now is the time to rest
simply and deeply on the currents of prayer, allowing the Spirit
to carry our spirit back to the One in whom we live and move
and have our being.

Obeying

The change that God is working deep into our souls will naturally flow outward into our lives, as surely as a river must follow its course to the open sea. In this remaining element of *lectio divina*, we contemplate the meaning of this word from God for the choices we will make this day, for the attitudes we will carry into our tasks, for the thoughts we will allow to dwell uppermost in our minds.

Now is the time to seek divine wisdom for carrying this precious gift into the flow of our life with God as it spills over into our life in the world—relationships with loved ones, interaction with friends, chance encounters with acquaintances, crossed paths with strangers. For example, we may find that the tenderness of Christ's word to Mary urges us to do a double take in offering a kind word of attention to those we might have overlooked, even to merely speak their name. We may feel so strengthened by God's awareness of us that we seek out a loved one to make sure that he or she is aware of our love and gratitude. The depth at which we have been touched gives us a fresh ability to see our circumstances in the light of what truly matters and attend to that, rather than allow ourselves to be pulled off center by peripheral distractions or false urgencies.

This process is sometimes called *application*. But there is a danger here. Application is often unfortunately reduced to steps on a to-do list in the latest program for spiritual self-improvement. Action steps may be good and helpful. But all too often they are used as a screen for resisting the actual work of spending time in the loving presence of God and surrendering to the deep inner change that is not so easily managed in controllable steps. Here again, when seeking the response of obedience, instead of working ourselves up into anxiety over "now what?" questions, we simply and quietly rely on the Spirit's lead.

The transformational power of *lectio divina* is on brilliant display in the life of a young man in northern Africa in the fourth century A.D. An earnest scholar in search of the good, the true, and the beautiful, Aurelius was living a deeply conflicted existence—devouring books by day and women by night. This double-minded collision of passions, aspiring to the highest while sinking to the lowest, drove him to a desperate search for resolution. One day he retreated to a small garden, tearing his hair out over the tumult in his heart:

> Then a huge storm rose up within me bringing with it a huge downpour of tears. . . . Suddenly a voice reaches my ears from a nearby house. It is the voice of a boy or a girl (I don't know which) and in a kind of singsong the words are constantly repeated: "Take it and read it. Take it and read it." At once my face changed, and I began to think carefully of whether the singing of words like these came into any kind of game which children play, and I could not remember that I had ever heard anything like it before. I checked the force of my tears and rose to my feet, being quite certain that I must interpret this as a divine command to me to open the book and read the first passage which I should come upon. . . . I snatched up the book, opened it, and read in silence the passage upon which my eyes first fell: "Not in rioting and drunkenness, not in chambering and wanton-

ness, not in strife and envying; but put ye on the Lord Jesus Christ, and make not provision for the flesh in concupiscence." I had no wish to read further; there was no need to. For immediately [when] I had reached the end of this sentence it was as though my heart was filled with a light of confidence and all the shadows of my doubt were swept away.[8]

Doubtless you have recognized this well-known event from the life of Aurelius Augustine, Bishop of Hippo and formative theologian in Christian history. It is a dramatic instance of the power with which God can speak to us through Scripture, catching us up into a deeper life with God and redirecting the course of our lives.

Do you see how "obedience" occurred here? Augustine did not whip out Paul's letter to the Romans, read through a portion of it quickly to check off his Scripture quotient for the day, and choose an application step, gritting his teeth while vowing, "I will *not* sleep with my girlfriend tonight." No, he was in earnest to hear a saving word from God for the sake of his life. As he responded to the urgent call to pick up the Bible and read, he opened himself to the flow of God's Spirit into his mind and heart and soul.

Now, we must not think that this story means that *lectio divina* always yields a life-shaking experience—but we may be sure of our continual need for life-changing encounters with God. Each and every day, whether we are pacing like a caged animal in desperation or yawning over a cup of coffee in a morning lull, there are high stakes involved in how we approach the Scripture.

Always, we are answering the question in one direction or the other: will we live with God, or without God? Ours is a with-God life and we must choose: God is with us—will we be with God?

Remember, even the slightest shift of our heart in obedience to the "still, small voice" of God can be just as radical as Augustine's conversion in its power to reshape us into the likeness of Christ. This transforming dynamic of God's Word is a sure promise to us:

> For as the rain and the snow come down from heaven,
>> and do not return there until they have watered the earth,
> making it bring forth and sprout,
>> giving seed to the sower and bread to the eater,
> so shall my word be that goes out from my mouth;
>> it shall not return to me empty,
> but it shall accomplish that which I purpose,
>> and succeed in the thing for which I sent it. (Isa. 55:10–11)

READING WITH BOTH HEART AND MIND

When a member of the religious establishment asked Jesus to name the greatest commandment among the hundreds upon hundreds in the Jewish Law, Jesus responded. "'You shall love the Lord your God with all your heart, and with all your soul, and with all your mind.' This is the greatest and first commandment" (Matt. 22:37).

When we come to the Bible with the mind only and not the heart, we separate the written word from the revealed Word—

Jesus Christ. This is the failure of biblicism, a form of faith in the Bible alone that leads to dangerous and harsh consequences. It is also the failure of radical secularism, a willful refusal to bracket out presuppositions and engage the Bible on its own terms. God will not serve our favorite orthodoxy. When we continually attempt to make the Bible serve our own agendas—and in doing so, distance ourselves from God—*lectio divina* is a way of recovering our ability to be attentive to the heart of God in the Word of God.

However, approaching the Bible with the eyes of our heart without our presence of mind will clutter the path with needless misunderstanding. Bringing our cognitive understanding to the revelation of Scripture is a way of obeying the greatest commandment to love God with all our heart and soul and mind. It would be presumptuous to assume that we can discern "what the Bible is saying" entirely on our own. We need a balanced approach to our intake of Scripture: heart, soul, mind.

One helpful way to describe this balance is with the theological formulation of the "Wesleyan quadrilateral" of Scripture, reason, tradition, and experience.[9] The next two chapters will offer specific ways of reading the Bible with the mind and in the context of the People of God—reason and tradition. Remember, always the goal is entering the transforming presence of Christ: "Beyond the sacred page I seek Thee, Lord; my spirit pants for Thee, O living Word."[10]

5

Reading with the Mind

Then he opened their minds to understand the scriptures.
—Luke 24:45

If we stand very close to a mosaic, we will see little pieces of whatever makes it up—pebbles, chunks of glass, shards of pottery, bits of metal. As we back away from it, looking at more of the whole instead of scrutinizing the parts, we will experience a moment in which the image created by all these little pieces suddenly "pops" out of the background into our vision. *Oh, now I see it!* we exclaim.

This is the moment of perception underlying Gestalt psychology, which theorizes that we are hardwired to recognize a unified and meaningful "whole" we can't distinguish simply by calculating the sum of all its parts. We will still see a triangle, for example, even if sections of its three sides have been erased. An illustration common among Gestalt theorists features a black-and-white picture that at first looks to be an abstract design of dots and squiggles. Before long, the average human eye recognizes in it trees, grass, and a Dalmatian dog sniffing the ground.[11]

This sudden clarity in perceiving an object or pattern is said to be evidence that inwardly we have been scanning for this "gestalt."

Taking in separate bits and pieces of the Bible for information alone is like examining the discrete parts of a mosaic before recognizing its overall design. The Christian understanding of God affirms that we have been divinely wired for relationship with God—and that in Christ, God has come seeking us. Therefore, when we come to the Bible with an open heart and an open mind, we can expect the sudden clarity of recognizing the living God who calls to us through its pages.

In the wake of the violence of the Bolshevik Revolution, a member of the Russian Imperial Diplomatic Corps emigrated with his family to Paris. His teenage son found himself adrift in the sudden shift from fighting hardship and danger to the relative ease of safety and peace. Happiness seemed meaningless if there was no purpose behind it. He decided that if he did not discover a meaning for his life within the next year, he would commit suicide.

As he neared the end of the year with nothing to show, the young man was asked to attend a lecture by a Christian speaker. He did not believe in God and had absolutely no use for the Church, and the lecture did nothing to change his convictions. Angry at what he had heard, he went home and asked his mother for a Bible so that he could check to see if the Gospels truly supported these views or not. He chose to read the Gospel of Mark because it had the fewest chapters and he did not want to waste any unnecessary time. He was in for a surprise:

I do not know how to tell you of what happened. I will put it quite simply and those of you who have gone through a similar experience will know what came to pass. While I was reading the beginning of St Mark's gospel, before I reached the third chapter, I became aware of a presence. I saw nothing. I heard nothing. It was no hallucination. It was a simple certainty that the Lord was standing there and that I was in the presence of him whose life I had begun to read with such revulsion and such ill-will. . . . This was my basic and essential meeting with the Lord. From then I knew that Christ did exist. It was in the light of the Resurrection that I could read with certainty the story of the Gospel, knowing that everything was true in it because the impossible event of the Resurrection was to me more certain than any event of history.[12]

This was the "gestalt" of Father Anthony of Sourozh, who established the Russian Orthodox diocese of Great Britain and Ireland. Although he was not looking for Jesus when he went to the Bible, he found him nonetheless—or perhaps more accurately, Jesus found him. He was examining the "pieces" of the Bible's witness to Christ, but it was the reality of the risen Christ that revealed God to him and enabled him to read the rest of the Scriptures in relationship to this central reality.

READING WITH UNDERSTANDING

"Any fool can know; the point is to understand," Albert Einstein is reported to have said. Reading the Bible for life with God is not

a matter of accruing information, but an act of genuine understanding empowered by the Holy Spirit. We are learning to love
God with the mind.

When Jesus is asked to name the greatest commandment, he
responds, "You shall love the LORD your God with all your heart,
and with all your soul, and with all your mind" (Matt. 22:37).
Jesus is quoting from Deuteronomy 6:5, but he changes it ever so
slightly, adding "mind" in place of "might." Hebrew tradition
has always placed high value on the right use of the mind, and
Jesus is here underscoring that reality.

Right reason is important in our handling of the Bible. Resources such as handbooks, Bible encyclopedias, and the like can
help bridge the millennia of history so that reading the Bible is
not an exercise in misreading the Bible. We use the tools of grammar, logic, historical context, modern critical research, the best
commentaries and exegetical scholarship—all of these are valuable to our task of reading the Bible. This, in part, is how we love
God with our minds. Of course, we are always learning to descend with the mind into the heart—we do not settle for understanding with the mind alone, but neither do we leave the mind
behind when we engage the Scriptures at the level of the heart.

The more we come to the Scriptures—internalizing them, dis-
covering the intent of the original authors, wrestling to compre-
hend the collective unity of the Bible's different parts—the more
readily we will be able to see the whole Story of redemptive history emerging from the mosaic-style background of the Bible's
contents. The unseen vessels of original documents and oral traditions are reflected in the Bible's shards of history. These chronolo-
gies glimmer with prisms through which we view God's intent

for human history in the multiple facets of prophetic and apocalyptic revelation. Interspersed throughout the Bible are nuggets of poetry, many of them gathered into prayer books of worship and praise. The shimmer of precious metals signals the treasures of wisdom literature, cut through with the broken-glass edges of argument, protest, and lament. Yet even suffering and injustice cannot lessen the heat of love's passion in the erotic literature of Song of Songs, nor dim the fierceness with which the Light of the world burns through the Gospel narratives and spreads throughout the epistles into the dark places of human history.

When we read the Bible in the context of redemptive history, it is no dry, academic exercise in amassing knowledge, but a dramatic plunge into a journey of understanding that is both edifying and disturbing. Our human reference points no longer apply.

The religious professionals of Jesus' day were blind to their true place in God's redemptive history because they devoted themselves to performance—to amassing knowledge and behaving in a way that was calculated to bring them praise for acquiring and applying such knowledge. It was a dry, lifeless process, not a journey of understanding, because it was devoid of the living Author. The text was the only authority. Failing to see the living God, they also failed to see themselves as they really were—people in need of the Messiah, called to live out the love and mercy of God. While the religious elite largely remained blind to Jesus, the truly needy of Jesus' day were able to see the Lord against the background of this simple carpenter from Nazareth whose teachings and ministry were unlike any other person they had ever met.

Today, we have the completed testimony of the written word to illuminate our understanding. Above and beyond all our human ideas about God stands the divine testimony of the Scriptures—a bulwark against the distortions of our imagination, a defense against our attempts to remake God in our own image. The Bible tells us what God is like. If we neglect its witness, as Dallas Willard warns, the consequences are serious, indeed:

> Failure to know what God is really like and what his law requires destroys the soul, ruins society, and leaves people to eternal ruin: "My people are destroyed for lack of knowledge" (Hosea 4:6), and "A people without understanding comes to ruin" (4:14). This is the tragic condition of Western culture today, which has put away the information about God that God himself has made available.[13]

God's active presence helps us understand the foundational meaning of the Scriptures for our relationship with him. As Jesus prepared to leave his disciples, he promised them, "I will ask the Father, and he will give you another Advocate [or *Helper*], to be with you forever. This is the Spirit of truth, whom the world cannot receive, because it neither sees him nor knows him. You know him, because he abides with you, and he will be in you" (John 14:16–17). This promise of the Spirit carried the assurance of guidance: "I still have many things to say to you, but you cannot bear them now," Jesus continued. "When the Spirit of truth comes, he will guide you into all the truth; for he will not speak on his own, but will speak whatever he hears, and he will declare to you the things that are to come" (John 16:12–13).

This promise of divine guidance has been understood by some of the old writers to mean that we have the ability to read the Bible and understand its message sufficiently to choose for or against belief in God. Each of us is accountable for that choice individually before God, not through family membership, religious authorities, or any other possible intermediaries. In response to religious tyranny, nineteenth-century Baptist writers developed this idea with the phrase "soul competency."[14] The assurance that God has given us full competency is a great liberation and should encourage ordinary folk to come to the Bible with confidence that God is with us and will guide us rightly in all things necessary to life. We may get plenty wrong, but we will get right what we need to get right.

For those times when we do get it wrong—and believe me, we will get it wrong at times—there are specific things we can do. Our comprehension is often limited by our lack of knowledge or hindered by personal agendas, clouded thinking, and misguided motives. If we come with humility of heart and mind, we have access to many ways in which we can check our understanding, interpretation, and application of the Scriptures. Educational references abound, as well as wise counsel, the indispensable benefits of reading and studying and hearing the Bible taught in community, the wisdom of Christian tradition, and more. These valuable resources can facilitate and confirm our hearing of the voice of God through the Bible. Of course, they are no substitute for the joy of discovery in reading the Bible ourselves.

We must understand that the Bible is an ancient text, and the unfamiliarity of its people, places, and events to contemporary eyes makes it seem far removed from our everyday experience. It takes effort to enter this strange new world of the Bible. For example, the Old Testament teaching of "life for life, eye for eye, tooth for tooth, hand for hand, foot for foot" (see Deut. 19:21; also Exod. 21:23–25) is often cited out of context to support capital punishment. However, if we research the historical context of this passage, we find that the ancient cultures surrounding Israel practiced retaliation, which involved escalating violence. The witness of God's people at that time was to limit the punishment to fit the crime and so avoid the tragic spirals of conflict. The intent of "an eye for an eye, a tooth for a tooth" was not to grant permission to "give as bad as you get," because Jesus corrected this misunderstanding by taking it to an even higher standard of turning the "other cheek"—bearing the strike without striking back. In his series of teachings on the Law, Jesus ushered in a new obedience that had more to do with the heart than with external observance of rules. He makes such declarations with the signature phrase, "You have heard it said . . . but I say to you . . ." (see Matt. 5).

We would do well to come to the Bible with these words ringing in our ears: *You have heard it said . . . but I say to you. . . .* Jesus ushered in a new way to read and understand the Scriptures because he was heralding the kingdom of God on earth: God with us.

The Immanuel Principle is the key to understanding the Bible's seeming lack of coherent organization. It does not present itself to us in a systematic, logical order. We balk at what seem to be inconsistencies or contradictions, because we think the Bible would be so much easier to understand if only it were arranged in logical compartments.

Reading with understanding enables us to see that the Bible could not do what it needed to do if it were laid out like a textbook. The Bible presents God's thundering invitation, "I am with you—will you be with Me?" Its order is shaped not by the progression of data, but by the idiosyncrasies of relationship. A depersonalized, antiseptic, perfectly ordered container is no vehicle for a love story. We look for perfect uniformity of telling, but the Bible is not a system of propositional truths detached from human experience. It is not a guidebook to religious life.

Does this mean that we will find ourselves frustrated by trying to wrap our minds around the Bible? No, not at all. It simply means that we adjust our mind-set to how the Bible tells us about itself. Above all it is a collection of stories, all testifying to one grand Story of a personal God in pursuit of relationship with human beings. So instead of asking why the Bible doesn't "make sense" the way we think it should, we ask, "How does the Bible tell its Story?"

HOW THE BIBLE TELLS ITS STORY

The Bible's witness to God's pursuit of human beings is a story of relationship, and therefore it is messy. It is not ordered by straight lines of logic, but meanders with the erratic circumstances of particular human beings who respond in differing ways to the call of God upon their lives.

Recounting the intertwined histories of families, tribes, and nations, the Bible goes forward and then circles back, takes detours and rabbit trails, leaves some parts out and tells others twice. It is chockful of details, some major, some minor, some puzzling and often astonishing—a patchwork quilt of vastly different times and places, of authors both known and anonymous. It tells stories that are clearly connected or strangely unconnected, about individuals as varied as hermits and harlots, mothers and mistresses ... those who are saints one minute and sinners the next. The Bible tells its story in communication styles as different as that of accountants from poets, single-minded leaders from visionary dreamers, scribal historians from apocalyptic seers.

We want neat, orderly systems; God gives us a koan: "I *am*." We want absolute truth nailed down in neat propositional form; the Bible gives us a vast sprawl of Divine-human history. We want bottom-line rules for life; the Bible gives us the law of love. We want programs to follow; the Bible tells us to follow hard after God. We want something tangible to show for our efforts; the Bible asks that we relinquish results and place our faith in what is unseen. The Bible reveals to us its Story—tragic as well as glorious, bloody and violent as well as nurturing and inspiring—by pouncing upon us from another realm, taking us by surprise.

To depict the Hound of Heaven tracking his beloved prey "down the nights and down the days ... down the arches of the years ... down the labyrinthine ways"[15] of human beings in their flight from God, how could one single form of telling possibly suffice? And so we have sweeping sagas of creation followed by plodding "begats" (genealogies)—because the grand drama never eclipses its cast of thousands. Each individual is as important as the next, despite the varying natures of their roles. Names are critical, and the Bible lists plenty of them to honor the memory of those who played a part in this Story, showing how this drama extends from face to face, from generation to generation. We stumble over the numbers of Numbers, yet they are there to bear witness to the particular history of a particular people in particular times and particular places.

We have the laws and the commandments for God's people, the histories of battles and rulers and families, the stories of heroes and heroines, the accounts of treachery and betrayal. But names and numbers and times and places and even grand stories are not enough to portray God's pursuit of human beings, for we must learn about God up close, not from a distance. Only poetry and prayer and the prophets' cries and whispers can express such wondrous intimacy in disclosing the loving heart of God. Only the words that pass directly between human soul and Divine Spirit can help us understand how to take off our shoes as we enter holy ground, how to cultivate friendship with God.

Yet even those words are still not enough to show the ways of God with human beings, and so the Bible records how God himself became one of us—so that we might see him in the flesh, feel his healing touch, watch him live and die and live again. The Bible makes sure we have direct, eyewitness testimony to this astonishing event, so that without seeing and touching and watching Jesus in earthly form we, too, may believe that he is alive and dwells among us.

The Bible's central Story is about relationship, and so for guidance in following Jesus it gives us not a book of morals or seven steps to self-help, but a slew of letters. They flow between people charged with spreading the Gospel—specific people with specific struggles. This is what it looks like to solve such dilemmas in a

Christlike way, we learn. These are the choices in following Jesus through alien and hostile societies, or within comfortable and complacent cultures. These are the big things on which you must stand firm, the letters say, and those are the little things you can let go. This is what it means to live for God's glory, whether you are on top or at the bottom of the social food chain, whether there is rain or sun, whether you feel strong or weak, whether you are married or single.

And finally the Bible concludes its Story not with an ending but with a new beginning. So vast and epic is this pursuit of God to form a people who perfectly give and receive love that it spills over into eternity. The Bible says that God has planted eternity in human hearts (see Eccles. 3:11) but how can eternity be conveyed to finite human minds? The biblical writers choose the most soaring imagery imaginable—a lamb enthroned who outshines the stars . . . a holy city made of precious gems, with a river of crystal flowing in its midst (see Rev. 21–22). How gracious God is to pull the veil aside and give us glimpses of the glories to come—a future beyond our wildest dreams, a Story beyond all telling.

SEEING OUR STORIES WITHIN THE BIBLE'S STORY

We are fortunate to have many different access points in the Bible for recognizing our stories within God's Story. Commenting on the literary variety of the Hebrew Scriptures, Peter Gomes observes, "Scripture is always understood to be a human response to the initiative of God." Whether the form is law, history, poetry, or wisdom, "the subject is always the same: the relationship between God and God's people."[16] The categories of Bible literature reflect the culture and worldview of their time and authorship, but each type offers a unique perspective on the narrative arc of divine mediation and human transformation—and therefore a unique perspective on how we find our place in it.

"Love God with all your mind." One practical way to do this is to become so familiar with the genres of Scripture that we can reach each one with appreciation for how it fits into the mosaic of the Bible's design—all the time remembering that the goal is not the mastery of the text, but the discovery of God through the text.

Law

The first literary form we encounter are the books of the Law— Genesis, Exodus, Leviticus, Numbers, and Deuteronomy. These five books comprise the Jewish "Torah," from a Hebrew word meaning "teaching" or "instruction," yet they cover far more than the codified system of rules and regulations prescribed for Hebrew life during the time of Moses. Beginning with creation accounts and God's activity in early human history, they describe how God establishes the nation of Israel as a people called forth and singled out to live in relationship with the one true God.

When the Israelites are subjugated and enslaved, in utter grace God stretches out a mighty hand to deliver them from bondage and lead them into new life in the land of promise. Then, having delivered them, God makes a covenant with them to bind them in relationship forever. The books of the Law spell out the details of this covenant.

Comprising more than six hundred commandments for worship, civic life, and moral standards, the covenant laws provide Israel with clear directions for living: obeying God's instruction, exhibiting God's love, expressing God's righteousness. Understanding how these laws would set apart Israel from the surrounding nations requires us to be familiar with the pagan cultures of the day. Only in that context can we begin to see how the law was not a burden to the people, but a gift to keep them in relationship with a holy God.

As we read the narrative of Israel's history in the books of Law, we can see how it illuminates our own drama of relationship with God: freedom versus bondage; trust versus fear; faithfulness versus disobedience; life ordered by relationship with God versus life disordered by broken relationship with God.

What, then, do the rules and rituals and festivals mean for us today?

First, we can see the relevance of these commandments in their detailed relation to every aspect of individual and community life and worship. Their very comprehensiveness indicates that God is involved in every aspect of human existence. Life with God will overflow any attempt to compartmentalize or contain it. It is not just for those who are "spiritually inclined." We are made to live with God at the very center of our lives, transforming our thoughts, actions, decisions, relationships, vocations, communities, and social structures.

Second, we can understand the relevance of God's commandments through recognizing them as a gift for enabling the people to maintain relationship with God—and for nations outside of God's People to find the way to the one true God. The people do not earn their place in God's covenant by obedience; rather, their obedience enables them to experience life with God. The sacrificial system is given not because God is keeping some divine bank account of blood money, which needs regular deposits to ward off divine judgment. Rather, it provides a way for the people to "come clean" whenever they break the covenant by disobeying God. Instead of punitive reprisal, they experience gracious restoration of the relationship. This is why the Law becomes such a source of joy, as we see in their celebrations and in the praise of the psalmists in the prayer book of the people.

We can read the books of Law for spiritual transformation by asking, "How can I live my life in a way that is faithful to God's covenant relationship with me?" For Christians, this does not mean that we follow Old Testament laws. It does mean that we learn God's law of love in Christ and seek to live in faithfulness to it.

History

The next twelve books of the Bible, Joshua through Esther, are commonly grouped under the heading of history, although this term is not precisely accurate in describing the literary forms of these books. The first nine, through Second Chronicles, pick up the history of Israel after entering the Promised Land. The last three—Ezra, Nehemiah, and Esther—recount specific stories of those dispersed by exile; some returning from Babylonian captivity, some still scattered in ancient Persia.

When the book of Joshua begins, the time of the so-called patriarchs (Abraham, Isaac, and Jacob) has now given way to a period of tribal confederation (the twelve tribes of Israel, from Jacob's twelve sons). The first three books of history—Joshua, Judges, and Ruth—recount how the baton of leadership passes from Moses' hand to Joshua's, and then to a succession of judges who preside over the people. God is with them through their struggles and triumphs in becoming a people with a specific place, through military campaigns and insurrections, rededications and pilgrimages.

As the Israelites grow increasingly restless for a king to rule over them, like the kingships of surrounding nations, their loose tribal confederation yields to nation building capped by the establishment of a monarchy and a succession of kings. The middle six books of "history"—the two-volume books of Samuel, Kings, and Chronicles—reveal God's transforming work in the blood, sweat, tears, and dust of entangled political, military, and social structures. Key figures emerge—the prophet Samuel; Saul, the first king; David, whose glorious reign included preparations for building the Temple, and whose intensity led him into grievous sin as well as extraordinary devotion to God; and Solomon, who completed the Temple and reigned with great wisdom before the temptations of wealth and power began leading him astray. The Bible has no tendency to extol perfect heroes. God alone is worthy of worship, and his chosen rulers are as vulnerable to moral failure and spiritual unfaithfulness as the people they govern. The history of God's people is a triumphal testimony to God's faithfulness alone.

And neither are these historical accounts written to provide exact chronological records: their purpose is to show how God continues to mediate his presence in order to transform the people of God into a community of love, whose lives will express this love and make it known throughout all the earth. We enter into this drama of transformation by seeking to understand how this history of God's chosen people reframes our view of our own history with God.

Reading the books of history through the lens of the with-God life shows us that beyond the families who birthed and raised us, we have an ultimate family of origin in the gracious love of God. The specific circumstances of our lives neither define our identity nor determine our destiny. Just as the Israelites' flawed personal history—beautiful and bloody, inspiring and ignoble—is eclipsed and transformed by God's divine history, so our personal stories are caught up in the greater Story of God's transforming work with humanity and creation. The Bible reveals our true past and forecasts our true future. Our lives have meaning far beyond the sum of our fleeting hours, days, and years.

Poetry and Wisdom Literature

Some of the most beautiful passages in literary history can be found in the books of Job, Psalms, Proverbs, Ecclesiastes, and Song of Solomon (also called Song of Songs). These are conventionally referred to as the books of Wisdom. A significant portion of the Bible is written in poetic form. In part, this may have aided the memorization and retelling of the people's sacred heritage in the oral tradition. These "Wisdom" books convey the deep beauty and mystery of God's involvement with his people. They carry the flights of the human heart in response—whether soaring in rapture or diving into despair.

The emotional immediacy of these books draws us with compelling force into the most intimate joys and sufferings of the human soul. Transformation virtually leaps from these pages as we journey with Job through the depths of human misery into the mystery of God's sovereignty . . . with the psalmists through the passions of the human soul into the enormous passions of a God who longs to dwell among us . . . with the writers of Proverbs and Ecclesiastes as they mine the ordinary for the treasures of wisdom and plumb the depths of experience in seeking answers to life's greatest questions . . . with the lovers in Song of Solomon as they dance the steps of arousal, intimacy, and ecstatic union.

For centuries, the People of God have experienced vicarious transformation by making these books their own journals and prayer books of devotion to God. For example, reading and chanting the psalms aloud, individually and in community, as part of a daily practice of fixed-hour prayer has been a practice across centuries of Christian history, taking the People of God through the entire Psalter in cycles of worship and prayer tied to seasons of the liturgical year. Others find that the thirty-one chapters of Proverbs lend this book to monthly reading cycles, one chapter per day. The melancholy poignancy and timeless resonance of Ecclesiastes has planted its words throughout classical and popular literature and song. And the luscious imagery of Song of Solomon has forever linked the spiritual and the erotic with exquisite unity.

Reading these books for spiritual transformation can be as simple as savoring them with a prayerful spirit, allowing them to give voice to our own deepest yearning, anguish, and joy. They will lead us into the holy place for which our spirits instinctively long, for, as Eugene Peterson says, "The Scriptures, read and prayed, are our primary and normative access to God as he reveals himself to us. The Scriptures are our listening post for learning the language of the soul, the ways God speaks to us; they also provide the vocabulary and grammar that are appropriate for us as we in our turn speak to God."[17]

Prophecy

A fourth category of Old Testament literature, prophecy, discloses to us voices of divine lament for our waywardness. The individual prophets—the "major" figures of Isaiah through Daniel and the "minor" figures of Hosea through Malachi—are sent at different times and in varying contexts. They speak for God in particular circumstances of national decay, exile, captivity, and oppression. When the nation of Israel is still united, the prophets function in dual roles of prophet and priest, or prophet and judge, providing guidance and correction to the king. Later, when the kingdom divides and the rebellious political structures of the people are no longer under their guidance and influence, the prophets become outsiders, in conflict with the institutions of power. They interpret God's action through circumstances of great suffering, declaring God's judgment on individuals and on the state, warning of imminent collapse and bondage, and calling the people to radical repentance.

Today, we often link the word *prophet* to *seer*, meaning someone who is able to see into the future and predict coming events—and the prophets certainly do that. However, the biblical understanding of prophets is not so much *fore-tellers* as *forth-tellers*. This calling involves speaking truth into the lives of the people, calling them back to their covenant obligations of single-hearted obedience to God, mercy and compassion for the poor and dispossessed, and justice and *shalom* toward all peoples.

The prophets speak some of the most tender and mournful words of love in all of the Bible. They call out to us as the People of God, reminding us of God's passionate love for us, of God's desire to dwell with us in faithfulness and intimacy, of God's sorrow when we quench the Spirit and turn away attempting to live on our own, apart from God.

Through the prophets, we see the covenant promises of God in new and rich ways, as God makes known the divine plan not only for the Israelites, but for all nations of the earth—indeed, for the whole creation—"For I am about to create new heavens and a new earth" (Isa. 65:17). We also witness the fury of God when human disobedience and predatory evil result in the people's unfaithfulness as a covenant partner: "I trod them in my anger and trampled them in my wrath; their juice spattered on my garments, and stained all my robes. For the day of vengeance was in my heart, and the year for my redeeming work had come" (Isa. 63:3–4).

As we read the Prophets, seeking to love God with our minds, we can ask God to lead us into the light of truth, revealing to us the ways in which we depart from it for our own agendas, exposing the idols we construct, convicting us of the ways in which we fail to seek mercy and justice for the poor and oppressed. We can listen for the voice of the One who calls us back into the righteous and just life of relationship: wooing, chastening, scolding, begging—but always, always pursuing.

The Deuterocanonicals

The body of writings commonly known as "the Apocrypha" is also known as the Deuterocanonical, or "second canon," writings. These books of law and history, wisdom writings, and prophetic and apocalyptic literature cover the period between our Old and New Testaments. Most of Christian tradition throughout history has accepted the Deuterocanonicals as part of the canon, though not giving these writings the same authority as Scripture—this is especially true for Protestants, many of whom do not include the Deuterocanonicals in their Bible.

The Deuterocanonicals deal with an important period in Israel's historical and spiritual development and contain many helpful insights for spiritual formation. The people Jesus encountered and taught were in many ways spiritually formed by these writings. In addition, these writings can function for us in much the same way that good sermons and devotional writings do. They provide ways in which we can understand our tradition as the People of God experiencing God's presence among us and following God's guidance in all walks of life.

Gospels and Acts

The story of how God has acted in human history shifts from the revelation of God through the Jews to the revelation of God himself in the Messiah, Jesus Christ. Here is the high watermark of divine revelation. The New Testament begins with the four Gospels and the book of Acts, which recount this dramatic new event in salvation history, the coming of Immanuel ("God with us"), and the spreading of the good news of Jesus Christ from the Jews to the Gentiles as the early Christian community takes form.

The Gospels introduce us to the majestic teachings of Jesus Christ. Here the brilliance of Jesus' words and actions catapult us into the life that is Life indeed, and that more abundantly (John 10:10). Through the dynamic use of parables, sermons, and proverbs we learn deeply and fully what it means to live with-God. Even more, by himself coming as incarnate Lord, Jesus ushers us completely into the with-God life, a life that is in and through him who is "the way, and the truth, and the life" (John 14:6). Here it is absolutely clear what "spiritual formation" is all about: disciples are "to obey everything that I have commanded you," and to teach others to do the same (Matt. 28:20). Obedience means to bring our inner person into such a transformed condition that the deeds of Christ naturally arise out of it. In a word, spiritual formation is "Christlikeness" from the inside out. It is this end to which God has been working since the beginning.

After the Gospels comes the book of Acts, a continuation of the acts and teachings of Jesus through the Holy Spirit (Acts 1:1). It displays in bold relief the great variety of Christian experience: from speaking in tongues and baptism by fire to logical analysis and philosophical debate (see Acts 2:1–3; 17:16–34). We see the dramatic unfolding of life with God, the breathtaking works of healing, evangelism, and demonic encounter, the infinite variety of ways in which we are called to the with-God life, and much, much more. All of this is through the dynamic power of the Holy Spirit, as God's ways are spread throughout the world in creating an all-inclusive community that leads the Jewish people beyond their ethnic identity to full identity as the universal People of God.

The Gospels and Acts surge with the transforming power of Christ as divine life washes like a mighty wave into every dusty corner of human existence. The question for each one of us is clear—will we follow Christ and become more like him? Will we pursue our own kingdom of self-seeking power, or will we choose a supernatural life in God's kingdom?

Epistles

The largest portion of the New Testament comprises epistles—letters from Paul and others to new believers with theological instruction for life, practical advice, encouragement, and exhortation. Here is a rich repast for loving God with the mind as we learn how the People of God, scattered in diverse local settings, live in the heavenly kingdom and, transformed by the power of God, obey the commands of God, thus becoming the friends of God. These letters—from Romans through Jude—provide the practical wisdom necessary for life with God.

Reading the New Testament epistles for spiritual transformation leads us into their rich treasures of wisdom for *zoë*—spiritual, eternal—life. These are not manuals of self-help techniques, but pathways into becoming spiritually alive: here we learn that it is possible to be physically alive *(bios)* but spiritually dead *(thanatos)*. Only through the secret of our life hidden with Christ in God—the *zoë* life, eternal and uncreated, originating in God alone—can we access the hidden reservoir of God's love and power that will form us as disciples of Jesus, expressing his love and teachings through our own lives.

As the book of Acts introduced us to the new communities of believers, so the epistles initiate us into the varied ways of living in community. Through the history of the People of God, gathered in the bond of the Holy Spirit, we learn who we are and how we should live. Although there are exceptions, the rule for sustaining a life with God is through an active, living connection to a visible expression of the Body of Christ. The People of God form a living community of disciples who spread the Gospel of the kingdom throughout the world and provide mutual support as they learn to walk in the way of Jesus.

Spiritual community is not perfect, and there are limitations to being spiritually formed in a community of like-minded, though extremely different (and perhaps difficult) people. Therefore, the letters of the New Testament have much to say about the struggles of Christian community today, the promises and the perils of local expressions of the Body of Christ. Individual faith joined to a community of faith is meant to strengthen our relationship with God, not stifle our faith. The letters also give us a clear measure of a false spirit of Christian community: anything that stifles the life-giving power of Christ's love is against God.

Apocalypse

The Bible concludes with the pulsating drama of Revelation. This book is written in the genre of apocalyptic prophecy that infuses the Old Testament books of Ezekiel and Daniel, in particular. The cataclysmic clash between God and Satan, between good and evil, reaches a feverish pitch when Satan's great scheme to destroy Christ is thwarted (Rev. 12–18). As the drama moves toward its glorious conclusion, the new heaven and the new earth, God's ultimate intention of establishing an eternal relationship with us is fully revealed: "'See, the home of God is among mortals. He will dwell with them; they will be his peoples, and God himself will be with them;' . . . They will see his face, and his name will be on their foreheads. And there will be no more night; they need no light of lamp or sun, for the LORD God will be their light, and they will reign forever and ever" (Rev. 21:3; 22:4–5).

Revelation gives us a vision designed to provide comfort and strength when evil seems to run rampant. God does have a plan for the ultimate consummation of all things, for our eternal future with him and with one another.

Speculation regarding how to apply the complex, often fantastic imagery of Revelation to actual people, nations, and events has led to obsessive and an often narrow focus on the "end times." Preoccupation with the end of the world is not unique to Christian faith, as enduring fascination with the sixteenth-century figure of Nostradamus and other such "prophets" of the future indicates. Human history is replete with often tragic stories of groups of people following cultlike leaders claiming to know when and how the world will end. Jesus warned that no person knows the day or hour when God chooses to culminate earthly life as we know it (see Matt. 24–25).

This is not to say that scholarly study of Revelation and its apocalyptic imagery is unnecessary or unimportant, for such illumination greatly enriches our understanding of this vision God gave to the People of God through the Apostle John. However, we can seek to love God with all our mind by reading Revelation with this simple question: "What are the life-changing implications of this eternal perspective of my ultimate destiny as a member of God's all-inclusive community of love?"

THE COMPANY OF OTHERS

When we find our story in the Bible's Story, our life in God's life, we join the procession of God's People in the great transforming crucible of divine initiative and human response. This transformation is not a one-time conversion event, but a recurring experience of growth and change as each day, each hour, we make a choice for life or for death—turning toward God or away from God until "by turning and turning we come 'round right."

Here is a path for loving God with the mind: we read the Bible in earnest, not from a sense of religious duty but because we long to return again and again to the primal source for understanding what life with God is like. We read in the context of the Story that has the power to gather up our own stories within it and give them back to us changed, charged with powerful new meaning and purpose. We read to understand how we can respond to God's gracious invitation by saying with every aspect of our lives, "Yes, Lord, I want to be with You."

The Bible itself is not the whole of God's Story. It is the sacred witness to the living, ongoing Story we are invited to join—to help shape it and carry it forward to the glorious day when death and mourning and crying and pain are gone, for the "old order of things has passed away" (Rev. 21:4, NIV). Each one of us adds to it with the little life we bring into its great life, as drops of rainwater add to a rushing stream.

The infinity of ways in which human history merges into redemptive history infuses great beauty and variety into life with God. In God's gracious design for this life, we do not live it alone as separate pieces that will one day be put together. We are already part of a whole, living in dynamic relationship with one another as the People of God revealing the grand design of God—the formation of a perfectly loving community with Christ at the center. This is why it is so important to read the Bible in the company of the People of God, "until all of us come to the unity of the faith and of the knowledge of the Son of God, to maturity, to the measure of the full stature of Christ" (Eph. 4:13).

God's wondrous creation of the Body of Christ gives us not a set of beliefs to unite us, not a set of rules to conform us to one another, but a person in whose common likeness we are continually being formed and re-formed. Reading the Bible with one another in the Spirit of Christ is what protects us from being "tossed to and fro and blown about by every wind of doctrine, by people's trickery, by their craftiness in deceitful scheming" (Eph. 4:14).

The goal of reading the Bible for spiritual transformation is to be changed in order to experience more of life with God. This change occurs in the context of *community*. Nowhere in Scripture is it suggested that we are lone rangers in the spiritual life. Change occurs as we experience life with God and the realities of life with one another so that, "speaking the truth in love, we must grow up in every way into him who is the head, into Christ, from whom the whole body, joined and knit together by every ligament with which it is equipped, as each part is working properly, promotes the body's growth in building itself up in love" (Eph. 4:15–16). This unity in love is the end goal of life together, and so we come to the Scripture as the People of God.

6

Reading with the People of God

Once you were not a people,
    but now you are God's people;
once you had not received mercy,
    but now you have received mercy.
               —1 Peter 2:10

Reading the Bible with heart and mind comes to its fullness as we read the Bible with others, seeing it through their passion and perspectives. We learn that reading with genuine understanding leads naturally and appropriately to reading with the People of God.

I had a vivid experience of this connection a few years ago, during a time when I was becoming very aware of the mighty hand of God upon the Korean people. The explosion of Christian growth and missionary activity in Korea in the last hundred years is astonishing, even miraculous. One Korean proverb describes this small peninsula, battered by war and oppression and political division, as "a shrimp between whales"—the whales being China and Japan. You see, it is jut like God to take a country thought to be of little significance in the economy of nation-states and do something we can only look at in wonder and amazement.

The experience I refer to began at the start of a year in which I had undertaken an extended meditation on the story of the resurrection of Lazarus, including the events leading up to its shattering climax (John 11). There is so much to feed on in this one event that month after month I continued to dwell within it, marveling at its range of emotion, its theological depth, its dramatic tension.

Five months into that year, I traveled to Korea, still meditating daily on John chapter 11. Many and varied were my experiences in that trip: intensive times on a prayer mountain, special meetings along the DMZ, and myriad morning prayer gatherings.

Toward the end of my trip, a small congregation gave me a parting gift of twenty-four long-stemmed roses. The next morning as I sat down to read and to ponder again the story of the resurrection of Lazarus, I looked over at those roses lying on the coffee table. Already they were beginning to wilt. Then the *debar Yahweh,* the word of the Lord, came to me indicating that the Church in the West is very much like those roses—still some blossom showing but wilting because it has been severed from its roots.

I began to weep at the immense sadness of this reality, for I knew it to be so. But then I heard a word of hope: "I will raise up my Church!" Resurrection, just like in the story of Lazarus.

And then a further word: "For resurrection to come in fullness, the root system first needs to be reestablished." It was only then that I began to understand the connection between all my weeks and months of meditation on John 11 and all that I had been learning among the Korean peoples about a life of prayer. Prayer *is* the root system. And it is a life of prayer that needs to be reestablished in our lives. What we so desperately need today is not individualized prayer experiences that we can turn on or off at will like a faucet, but prayer as a constantly flowing life.

Then my mind was given understanding. God has sovereignly chosen to use the peoples of Korea to teach the worldwide Christian family about how to develop the root system of prayer. I speak here of both those in Korea and those of the Korean diaspora, both the Korea of the south and the Korea of the north. (Mark my word, God's revival visitation that began in the north, will, in God's time and in God's way, return in fullness to the north.)

Now, I am not being naïve here, or overly idealistic. I am fully aware of the inadequacies and weaknesses in the Korean prayer experience. Still, I believe God has chosen the Korean peoples to teach us about prayer as a constantly flowing life. There is something transcendent about Korean Christians at prayer. It is the intensity. It is the determined persistence. It is the instant power engagement. It is the longing love. It is the agony and the pain and the heartfelt sorrow. It is all of these, and more. It is a reality that cannot quite be reduced to words. It can only be received humbly through lived experience.

The experiences of my brothers and sisters in Korea enriched my understanding of the momentous events of John chapter 11. Reading the Bible with others does not mean only that we read together in a small group, or that we read commentaries to benefit from the wisdom of great teachers, or that we listen to the

Bible read and reflected on in worship or other gatherings. It also means reading the Bible through the lens of others' experiences, in the knowledge of others' stories, in the midst of immersion in others' lives. For all this is in the service of loving God and loving one another. It is not to make us more knowledgeable about the Bible's text, although that is helpful. It is not to make us more culturally sophisticated, although that is a benefit. It is to plunge us deeper into life with God, and therefore deeper into life with one another, that we might take one more step toward the beloved, all-inclusive community centered in Christ.

We read with others to feed our souls and activate our conscience, to be *formed, con*formed, and *trans*formed. This spiritual formation happens in the crucible of life together, as we follow the counsel of the writer to the Hebrews: "Let us consider how to provoke one another to love and good deeds, not neglecting to meet together, as is the habit of some, but encouraging one another, and all the more as you see the Day approaching" (10:24–25).

WE ARE ALL IN THIS TOGETHER

In the royal courts of Babylon and Persia, a Hebrew exile, Daniel, maintains unwavering obedience to God despite repeated attempts on his welfare and his life to make him renounce his faith. Yet it is this "Daniel in the lions' den," a model of absolute faithfulness, who pleads, "Ah, LORD, great and awesome God . . . we have sinned and done wrong" (Dan. 9:4). He is visited by the angel Gabriel "while I was speaking, and was praying and confessing my sin and the sin of my people Israel" (verse 20). The prophet Daniel calls upon the Lord's love for the people in his great prayer of confession, asking for release from oppression, even though he himself is innocent of the sins of idolatry that led to captivity by the Babylonians. Daniel identifies with his people. He does not stand outside of them, but inside the community, repenting on their behalf.

Daniel's generosity before the Lord speaks clearly that we are all in this together. Together we are part of holy history, members of a living community. Yes, we may be highly critical of the community, but we are always part of it.

There is no "us" and "them" in the way of Christ. God has called us as a people, God is gathering us as a people, and God is forming us as a people. As Peter affirms, we have received God's mercy in *becoming* a people (1 Pet. 2:10).

Remember that Peter is the most independent-minded disciple among the Twelve. Passionate and impulsive, Peter is the one who steps out onto the water and tries to walk to Christ. Peter, the lone ranger, draws a sword against those who come to arrest Jesus in the Garden. But the Spirit of Christ gives Peter life-changing lessons about the new community that is being formed with Jews and Gentiles alike. And when Peter writes his epistles to believers scattered throughout the Roman Empire, he pens one of the most beautiful passages in all of Scripture about the community of faith: "But you are a chosen race, a royal priesthood, a holy nation, God's own people, in order that you may proclaim the mighty acts of him who called you out of darkness into his marvelous light" (1 Pet 2:9). Life with God is, by definition, life in community.

Throughout Christian history, the Bible has been read in company with the historic witness of the People of God—"the communion of saints." We read the Bible in conversation with many others, including wise and mature interpreters of Scripture today. This corporate reading of the Bible illuminates for us the multifaceted ways the Immanuel Principle is experienced in ordinary life.

The Christian tradition derived its identity as the community that reads the Bible from the Hebrew concept of the synagogue as a center for worship and study. What the Church has historically understood to be the inspired and authoritative Scriptures has always formed the core of its worship, teaching, and sacraments. While the widespread availability of copies of the Bible has been a tremendous blessing, with it has come a tendency to personalize it as *my* Bible in a way that would have been foreign to earlier generations. As Anglican Archbishop Rowan Williams observes:

> Those of us who assume that the normative image of Scripture reading is the solitary individual poring over a bound volume, one of the great icons of classical Protestantism, may need to be reminded that for most Christians throughout the ages and probably most in the world at present, the norm is *listening*. . . . So the Church [reads Scripture publicly] not as information, not as just instruction, but as a summons to assemble together. . . . Whatever we do in private with our reading of Scripture, we must do in awareness of this public character.[18]

The People of God are an all-inclusive community, gathered in the power of God, filled with the love of God, and empowered to do the works of God. Their common sacred text is the Scripture. Wherever we are located within that all-inclusive community, we have the great privilege of seeing the Scripture through the eyes of the whole community. We can see the beautiful variety of ways in which the Bible has inspired and instructed the family of faith across generations and traditions. How boring life would be if we listened only to our own insights! How narrow our vision would be if we limited it only to our own understanding! How sad it would be if we missed out on what God has for all of us by failing to listen to how God speaks at various times and in various ways through parts of the whole. "There are many members, yet one body," Paul reminds us. "The eye cannot say to the hand, 'I have no need of you,' nor again the head to the feet, 'I have no need of you'" (1 Cor. 12:20–21).

As technology expands our global awareness and creates new opportunities for networks of instantaneous communication, we can see as never before how the winds of the Spirit blow across denominational divides, cultures and ethnicities, and geopolitical borders. Just as the Koreans have much to teach us about prayer, so the Africans have much to teach us about reconciliation, and the Chinese about faithful endurance through suffering and persecution, and the First Peoples of North America about the challenges of cultural hegemony to the universality of the Gospel.

To help us read the Bible in company with the diverse witness of the whole People of God, let me take you on a brief tour through the historic ways the Christian community has drawn from the Bible its understanding of the relational dynamics of life with God. These are all great historical traditions that can be seen throughout the centuries; they are also intimate dimensions of a personal spiritual life before God. These are all deeply rooted in the Scripture witness; they are also practical experiences of our own diverse, individualized spiritualities. By understanding something of the history and practice of these "Streams" we will be better able to enter the richness and diversity of the biblical witness. I mention six:[19]

- the *Contemplative* tradition, or "the prayer-filled life,"

- the *Holiness* tradition, or "the virtuous life,"

- the *Charismatic* tradition, or "the Spirit-empowered life,"

- the *Social Justice* tradition, or "the compassionate life,"

- the *Evangelical* tradition, or "the Word-centered life," and

- the *Incarnational* tradition, or "the sacramental life."

The Bible Teaches the Prayer-Filled Life

Imagine Jesus saying to you what he said to his disciples when they returned from a mission trip: "Come away to a deserted place all by yourselves and rest a while" (Mark 6:30). Now add this tender invitation: "Be still, and know that I am God!" (Ps. 46:10). You have entered the intimate place of drawing apart to become enveloped in the love of God. You are tasting the sustenance of the Contemplative tradition.

From the early-Church fathers and mothers who sought the stillness and clarity of the desert to contemporary men and women of prayer and action such as Frank Laubach and Henri Nouwen, the People of God have a rich tradition of drawing deeply from the well of God's love and entering into the intimacy of God's immediate presence. Theirs is a response to the Bible's call to "draw near to God" (Heb. 10:22, NIV). Seeking God in solitude and stillness, meditating on God's Word, and devotion to prayer are central to the life of the People of God, as we can see in the rich repository of the Psalms . . . the call of the prophets to repent in quietness and trust (Isa. 30:15) . . . Jesus' life of perfect unity with the Father . . . the devotion of the early believers to constant prayer (Acts 1:14) . . . the Apostle John's familiar intimacy with the love of God. The more we gaze upon God, the more of God's goodness and grace will permeate our life.

Examples of this stream flow throughout the Bible. The Psalter itself is a direct portal into this intimate focus on God—for example, Psalm 119 is a love letter to God based on an extended meditation upon God's Law. From his lonely vigil in the midst of a turbulent, danger-filled life, the prophet Elijah heard God's voice not in the earthquake, wind, or fire, but in a quiet whisper (1 Kings 19). Mary the mother of Jesus pondered the ways of God in her heart, and Mary of Bethany forsook all other tasks to sit at the feet of Jesus (Luke 2:19; 10:42). The Apostle John, whose epistles are brimming with the love of God in their insistence upon the primacy of love in our lives, called himself "the disciple Jesus loved" (John 20:2)—perhaps because his relationship with Jesus was so intimate that the love of God became the defining reality in his life.

To be sure, if we spent all our time in the Contemplative stream alone, it might carry us into an imbalance that would distance us from serious engagement with the pressing social issues of our day, isolate us from community, slight the intellectual dimension of faith, or elevate asceticism itself to an end instead of a means. But if we neglect the prayer-centered life, we risk forgetting our first love (Rev. 2:4). In the burning intensity of the desert, we can feel the heat radiating from the heart of God—and our heart will grow tender and warm in response.

We do not need a specialized vocation to be contemplative followers of Jesus. There are many ways to wade into the waters of the prayer-centered life—to start with, and to return to again and again, we have a lifetime of Scriptures in which to soak our mind, heart, and soul in drawing near to the loving heart of God.

The Bible Teaches the Virtuous Life

Have you ever heard the term *holiness* and thought of it as meaning "holier than thou"? Many people think being holy means being moralistic—preoccupied with rule keeping as a way of establishing personal righteousness, and judging how righteous other people are based on well they keep moral rules. After all, the Bible is filled with commands to holiness and moral perfection: "Be holy, for I am holy" (Lev. 11:44) . . . "Be perfect, therefore, as your heavenly Father is perfect" (Matt. 5:48) . . . we are "called to be saints" (1 Cor. 1:2) . . . "as he who called you is holy, be holy yourselves in all your conduct" (1 Pet. 1:15) . . . "whoever fears has not reached perfection in love" (1 John 4:18).

By the time of Jesus, the Jewish leaders—in particular, the Pharisees—had raised the practice of law keeping to virtual perfection. Yet Jesus says in the Sermon on the Mount, "Unless your righteousness exceeds that of the scribes and Pharisees, you will never enter the kingdom of heaven" (Matt. 5:20). Have we been given an impossibly high standard to live up to?

Jesus cuts through this dilemma in his warning to the Pharisees: "You are those who justify yourselves in the sight of others; but God knows your hearts; for what is prized by human beings is an abomination in the sight of God" (Luke 16:15). We are called to a holiness of the heart, not moral scrupulousness. Over and over again—from the circumcision of the heart and the sacrifices of a contrite spirit in the Old Testament; to Jesus' call to wholehearted life in the kingdom of God; to the New Testament epistles in their emphasis on the fruit of the Spirit and the outward testimony of a godly inward life—the Bible calls us to a transformation from within. Only a change of heart will shift our lives in the direction of God's holiness—the perfection of love and truth in which we are called to live and move and have our being (Acts 17:28).

The liabilities and strengths of pursuing the with-God life through the lens of the holiness tradition range along a spectrum of opposites, from externally driven performance to internally rooted desire:

- the *legalism* of focusing on rule keeping versus devoting ourselves to *loving* God and others;

- the attempt to *earn righteousness through works* (Pelagianism) versus seeking *growth in grace* through the process of human spirit cooperating with Holy Spirit;

- the temptation to seek *perfectionism* in behavior instead of *purity of heart* in desiring life with God above all else.

The holiness stream teaches us to rejoice in the sanctifying grace available to us in Jesus Christ. It yields the kind of joy that nineteenth-century revivalist Phoebe Palmer, who suffered through the tragic deaths of three children, experienced in her wondrous epiphany of complete surrender to the ways of God in her life: "... *I received the assurance that God the Father, through the atoning Lamb, accepted [my] sacrifice;* my heart was emptied of self, and cleansed of all idols, from all filthiness of the flesh and spirit, and I realized that I dwelt in God, and felt that he had become the portion of my soul, my ALL IN ALL."[20]

The Bible Teaches the Spirit-Empowered Life

From the moment of Jesus' baptism, when "the Holy Spirit descended upon him in bodily form like a dove" (Luke 3:22), until the moment of his death on the cross, Jesus was "full of the Holy Spirit" (Luke 4:1). Look up the word *Spirit* in reference to Jesus in the Gospels, and you will find many accounts of the Spirit in Jesus' emotional responses, decisions, and teachings. Does Jesus' experience seem impossibly beyond your reach? Then consider this invitation:

> [Jesus] cried out, "Let anyone who is thirsty come to me, and let the one who believes in me drink. As the scripture has said, 'Out of the believer's heart shall flow rivers of living water.'" Now he said this about the Spirit, which believers in him were to receive; for as yet there was no Spirit, because Jesus was not yet glorified. (John 7:37–39)

John records that Jesus stood when he issued this wondrous offer—the practice at the time was for teachers to sit while giving instruction, so think of the emphasis Jesus must have been giving this proclamation with his body language. This life is for you and for me. This is life in the Spirit, the birthright of all who choose to follow Jesus.

The New Testament, following the four Gospels, gives us specific understanding of how the Spirit of God empowers and gives life to the human spirit when we open ourselves to the Spirit's work. The great teachings of Paul in Romans 12, Ephesians 4, and 1 Corinthians 12–14 describe the *charismata,* or gifts of the Spirit, with which believers are endowed for the purposes of leadership, ecstatic empowerment, and community-building.[21] As we exercise these gifts in the power of the Spirit, rather than attempting to use them for our own purposes or to manipulate others, our lives will increasingly exhibit the fruit of the Spirit— love, joy, peace, patience, kindness, generosity, faithfulness, gentleness, and self-control (Gal. 5:22–23).

The charismatic tradition in church history, so brilliantly illuminated in the life and ministry of the Apostle Paul, has animated the People of God through leaders such as Gregory the Great, who launched the Gregorian liturgical movement at the turn of the seventh century; monastics in the Middle Ages such as Hildegard of Bingen and Francis of Assisi (both twelfth century); revival leaders in later centuries, such as Charles Wesley (eighteenth century) and Aimee Semple McPherson (early twentieth century); and contemporary leaders such as John Wimber and David Yonggi Cho.

If the charismatic stream is cut off from the other great streams of Christian life and faith, its imbalances can lead to distortions such as treating the spiritual gifts "magically" as ends in themselves rather than means to nurturing the life and witness of the Body of Christ; an overemphasis on emotional experience at the expense of intellectual clarity; a widening gap between the gifts of the Spirit and the fruit of the Spirit; and an exaltation of visions and prophecy, which sometimes manifests itself in obsession with speculating about apocalyptic scenarios.

If the charismatic stream is allowed to run dry, however, then we may find ourselves attempting to shrink God down to understandable and manageable size—but God's ways are not our ways (Isa. 55:8), and the Spirit blows where he wills (John 3:8). We might also find our experience of life with God dwindling down to too much talk, too little action—as Paul cautions, "The kingdom of God depends not on talk but on power" (1 Cor. 4:20). And tragically, we can be left to ourselves instead of experiencing the vitality and growth of genuine transformation in Christ. Life in the Spirit is what moves us to exclaim with the psalmist, "Whom have I in heaven but you? And there is nothing on earth that I desire other than you. My flesh and my heart may fail, but God is the strength of my heart and my portion forever" (Ps. 73:25–26).

The Bible Teaches the Compassionate Life

The prophet Micah was called to take a stand against the corruption of a dark time in the divided kingdoms (Israel to the north; Judah to the south). Deceitful rulers and false prophets preyed upon the People of God while posturing as their appointed spiritual leaders:

> Hear this, you rulers of the house of Jacob
> and chiefs of the house of Israel,
> who abhor justice
> and pervert all equity,
> who build Zion with blood
> and Jerusalem with wrong!
> Its rulers give judgment for a bribe,
> its priests teach for a price,
> its prophets give oracles for money;
> yet they lean upon the LORD and say,
> "Surely the LORD is with us!
> No harm shall come upon us." (Mic. 3:9–11)

Throughout the writings of the Prophets, God's severest judgment is reserved for those who try to cover their evil intent with the garb of religious vestments. Their brazen presumption spreads their immorality throughout social structures like a virus, infecting the entire community with oppression and injustice. Into this noxious environment Micah brings the word of the Lord like a fresh wind. God does not want the stench of "calves a year old" or "thousands of rams" by way of penance in burnt offerings. No, God is not interested in the people's religious rituals:

> He has told you, O mortal, what is good;
> and what does the LORD require of you

but to do justice, and to love kindness,

and to walk humbly with your God? (Mic. 6:8)

This is what the life looks like that God intends for them. *Shalom*—the social well-being and peace of those living in harmony with God and each other—is what characterizes the family dynamics of the loving community God is creating. This is the vision that has catalyzed believers across the centuries to champion the cause of the neglected and the oppressed: from the deacons of the early Church who practiced true religion by looking after widows and orphans (James 1:27) . . . to medieval monastics who gave rise to orders such as the Vincentians, devoted to acts of justice and charity . . . to Quakers in their crusades against slavery and violent conflicts . . . to modern-day saints such as Dorothy Day, Mother Teresa, and Rosa Parks . . . all have understood that walking humbly with God means walking deep into the suffering and distress of this world with mercy and love.

Doing justice and practicing loving-kindness are the relational dynamics ushered in by Jesus, the gold standard of leadership as it were: humble, sacrificial, loving service. In Jesus, *shalom* is now possible—in fact, with Jesus' arrival, God's kingdom has now been made available to all: "Repent, for the kingdom of God has come near," Jesus announced at the beginning of his ministry (Matt. 4:17). And what does the kingdom look like, which Jesus is heralding? Well, Jesus tells us exactly what it looks like throughout his entire ministry, in his actions and his teachings and especially in his parables—but we have a beautiful picture of it in the early announcement he makes in his home synagogue of

Nazareth, when he stands up and reads from the prophet Isaiah's vision of the Year of Jubilee:[22]

> The Spirit of the Lord is upon me,
> because he has anointed me
> to bring good news to the poor.
> He has sent me to proclaim release to the captives
> and recovery of sight to the blind,
> to let the oppressed go free,
> to proclaim the year of the LORD's favor. (Luke 4:18–19)

To the astonishment of all those present, after reading from the scroll Jesus declares, "Today this scripture has been fulfilled in your hearing" (Luke 4:21). The kingdom of God is like a perpetual Jubilee year. Jesus was delivering "a war cry of social revolution."[23] Debts would be forgiven, the land would be healed of exploitation and overuse, the imprisoned would be set free, and the economic scales would be reset in order to ensure just distribution of equity.

Any personal morality that does not include such *shalom* in the social order is not truly Christian morality, according to the social justice stream of Christian life and faith. This beautiful reality of a just and compassionate social order is what Jesus taught us to pray for. Consequently, Christians have been praying for this reality for over two thousand years, and will continue to do so until the Lord returns, each time the Lord's Prayer is said: "Your kingdom come. Your will be done, on earth as it is in heaven" (Matt. 6:10). Jesus was not giving us a bit of wishful thinking, or some lovely idea to emblazon on a wall hanging: he was calling us to enter into a *reality* he established for us by bringing together heaven and earth. Now, because of the Incarnation, the dwelling place of God truly is *with* human beings. In the life of the Spirit, we can enter into this reality of God's kingdom more and more, so that life in this world—not just the next—will become more like the life for which we were created.

If the dynamics of life with God are ordered around the compassionate life alone, the greatest danger is that social justice may become an end in itself, increasingly distanced from its origins in spiritual realities and the challenge of transforming the human heart, not just changing social structures and conditions. Another peril is its susceptibility to becoming invested in a particular political agenda, undermining its prophetic power to critique the kingdoms of this world by the standards of the kingdom of God. This co-opting can lead to judging others when positions on issues become more important than the mandates of the Gospel.

However, the compassionate life has power to keep us from withdrawing into a solipsistic spirituality by reframing our understanding of life with God in all its fullness:

- right living extends to the right ordering of the social sphere in all its dimensions;

- love seeks the well-being of others, not just at the individual level but also at the level of the social structures and authorities that oppress and exploit them;

- diversity—i.e., embracing "the other"—enriches human relationships and reminds us that the Body of Christ transcends all cultural presuppositions;

- personal ethics are intertwined with social ethics;

- the ideals of the kingdom are for this life, not just the next one.

Attending to the needs of others—whether in the physical, spiritual, social, or political spheres—is as central to Christian faith as the greatest commandment: "'You shall love the Lord your God with all your heart, and with all your soul, and with all your mind.' This is the greatest and first commandment. And a second is like it: 'You shall love your neighbor as yourself.' On these two commandments hang all the law and the prophets" (Matt. 22:37–40).

The Bible Teaches the Word-Centered Life

"In the beginning was the Word," writes the Apostle John, "and the Word was with God, and the Word was God. He was in the beginning with God. All things came into being through him, and without him not one thing came into being. What came into being in him was life, and the life was the light of all people" (John 1:1–4). This profound declaration animates the heart of the Evangelical tradition: Jesus, the Word living; the Scriptures that testify to him, the Word written; and the transforming message of the Gospel, the Word proclaimed.

Before Jesus' coming, the good news of God's kingdom had been mediated only through God's chosen people. Now, the door to this good news—that all people can become part of God's loving community, in this life now and in the life to come—is flung wide open as that community of perfectly loving persons is made visible in Jesus Christ. *This* is the life to which we are invited. *This* is what it looks like to have an abundant life with God. *This* is the way to find it, live in it, rejoice in it, and help bring others into it:

> It is not that God's kingdom of love did not exist before Jesus, or that it had been postponed somehow. No. But before the incarnation its availability had, in the nature of things, been restricted and mediated through a special people and a special religious class. In Jesus' person all that changed. In Jesus the doors were thrown wide open: "Whosoever will may come." The kingdom of God's love has been made available to all. Whenever, wherever, whoever. In Jesus' person.[24]

The historical roots of the Word-centered life stretch from the Apostle Peter's transformation from fear to boldness as a shepherd of the flock and a fisher of men and women; through Saint Augustine's startling "take and read" conversion when the Word of God seized him from a carnal life and plunged him into the cleansing stream of the godly life; to the "sola scriptura" rallying cry of the Protestant reformers; to the "come to the waters" call of the revivalists and missionaries in the great spread of Christian faith across the globe in the last two centuries.

The last half of the twentieth century saw the rise of the modern Evangelical movement, a highly visible expression of the historic Evangelical stream. Perhaps no Evangelical leader during that time has had more international visibility than the evangelist Billy Graham, whose life and ministry illustrate the great themes of this tradition. His stadium crusades around the globe and his communication through a variety of mass media have proclaimed the Gospel to millions. His single-minded focus on the love of God revealed in Jesus Christ, available to all who repent, has been the unwavering basis of all his messages. And his successful efforts to train itinerant evangelists has ensured continuity in the faithful interpretation of the Gospel, through conferences designed to train and equip Christian leaders at the grassroots level throughout the globe.

The Evangelical tradition is characterized by its fervor for a personal experience of conversion, by its insistence on biblical fidelity and sound doctrine, and by its urgent call to evangelism and discipleship for all believers. When any of these characteristics is allowed to dominate our understanding of life with God, however, it leads to an unhealthy narrowing of the Gospel. Without the balancing emphasis of social justice, focusing on personal experience can lead to an understanding of life with God that is vertical at the expense of the horizontal—so heavenly minded as to be of no earthly good. Without the inner richness of the contemplative life, focusing on sound doctrine may anchor faith in the head but not also in the heart. Without the charismatic appreciation for life in the Spirit and the wholehearted expression of the holiness stream, biblical fidelity can descend into a rigid biblicism—worship of the written Word instead of the living Word. And without the tempering of the sacramental life, evangelism and discipleship can be reduced to formulas for admittance to heaven instead of a call to a rich, God-soaked life.

The Bible Teaches the Sacramental Life

The sixth stream of understanding the relational dynamics of life with God takes the previous five and seeks to integrate them into the rhythms of daily life. This is the Incarnational stream: the embodied life with God.

The word *sacrament,* in its generic form, means an outward sign of an invisible grace. In its specialized usage, it refers to religious rituals with a God-invested power to transform those who participate in them sincerely. Various branches of Christendom differ in which sacraments are essential for the Church to perform, but all of them believe that these specific rituals were instituted by Jesus and Church practice for the life and worship of his followers. The two sacraments common to nearly all Christian faith traditions are baptism and communion, or the Eucharist.

To speak of life as "sacramental" means that everything visible in some way points to the invisible—in Christian understanding, the constant, upholding reality of eternal grace. The sacramental life sees the relational dynamics of life with God invoked in every moment of life. If we are truly alive to the manifest presence of the living God, even the most ordinary of experiences can become an extraordinary experience of grace. A bird in flight can become a herald of the movement of the Spirit. Looking steadily into the face of another person can become an experience of looking into the face of God. An empty bowl placed on a homemade altar can become an icon of spiritual poverty. A walk in the woods can lead us to see, smell, and feel the glory of God in the land of the living. Shopping in a lavishly stocked grocery store can become an epiphany of gratitude for abundance—or of godly sorrow for those without access to, or money for, fresh water and nourishing food.

In his life on earth, Jesus forever rooted the life of holiness in the dust and sweat of human existence. God did not show up among us in a miraculous breakthrough of chariots through the clouds, descending amid spectacular fanfare to command our attention and worship. No. God showed up in the most ordinary and common way possible, from the ground up, in an out-of-the-way place, with only a few common folk summoned to witness his arrival. Jesus *grew up* among us. He began his life as a crying baby, like all the rest of us. Most of his years on earth were spent in ordinary human activities—attending synagogue, obeying his parents, learning his lessons, apprenticing in the carpentry trade. Only a tenth of his time was given to revealing his identity as the Messiah and engaging in ministry. The other nine-tenths were not "lost years" simply because the Bible gives only a few glimpses of what went on during them. Jesus was growing in wisdom, "and in divine and human favor" (Luke 2:52).

The Bible shows us that God works through long periods of our lives in which—apparently—nothing much seems to happen. We are familiar with Moses' awesome enactments of God's liberation, and his grand encounters with God in the burning bush and at the top of Mount Sinai. However, we don't pay much attention to the forty years he spent herding sheep in the wilderness before God called him to lead the Israelites out of slavery. Fourteen thousand, six hundred days of birthing lambs, warding off predators, moving skittish animals from field to field, butchering and eating them, shearing and selling their wool . . . day in and day out, season after season . . . seems like a very long time to "wait" on God. Yet that is what Moses experienced, for a good chunk of his life, as life with God.

Such "downtime" might easily be overlooked and undervalued if we viewed life with God only through the lenses of the other traditions of Christian faith. The Incarnational tradition grounds us in life with God by affirming *every* aspect of human experience as potentially holy ground. Material reality is not the opposite of spiritual reality, but the vehicle through which that reality becomes visible. This is why you will find, in some congregations, worship that involves all five senses with objects that represent hidden realities: beautiful images, whether stained-glass windows, a carefully woven stole, an icon of a saint, or a finely sculpted ceramic chalice . . . the fragrant aroma of incense . . . the sounds of chanting and music alternating with silence . . . the touch of human hands surrounding the taste of bread and wine. But it is also why you will find, in some retreat centers, the most elemental components in an environment designed to facilitate a sense of God's immediate presence: wood, stone, water, landscape, and the sacrament of taking God in—literally—through earthly things, the hallowed fruits of field and vineyard.

The great strength of the Incarnational tradition is that it awakens us to the sacrament of the present moment—whether doing dishes in the kitchen, as Brother Lawrence experienced while practicing the presence of God; or suffering in a Russian gulag, as Aleksandr Solzhenitsyn endured; or reading a short story by Flannery O'Connor, a writer of startling and earthy clarity in exploring all things spiritual; or reminding children to pick up their clothes while trying to get the laundry put away before leaving for soccer practice; or showing up at work to perform the same tasks we carried out yesterday, and the day before, and the day before that.

A liability of the Incarnational tradition is that in focusing on the visible means of grace, we can gradually distance ourselves from the invisible by forgetting that the material is a portal only, not the destination. Or we can become so enamored with symbols and rituals that we turn them into idols of our attention. We can grow precious about our ways of worship, insisting that others agree with us about their theological significance. We can become addicted to a certain kind of experience, demanding it as the only way we can enter into a felt sense of God's presence. We can become so preoccupied with "doing" the present moment that we forget what we are "doing" it for.

In its fullest expression, the sacramental life is summed up in Paul's words, "And whatever you do, in word or deed, do everything in the name of the Lord Jesus, giving thanks to God the Father through him" (Col. 3:17). This is a good example of taking the Bible literally!

FREEDOM TO DISAGREE

"[Bear] with one another in love, making every effort to maintain the unity of the Spirit in the bond of peace," Paul instructs us (Eph. 4:2–3). Our natural tendency is to assume that our particular way of reading the Scripture is the most accurate way, and everyone else is still in need of enlightenment. Learning to bear with one another in love means learning to allow one another the freedom to follow the leading of the Spirit.

The same Bible that in early twentieth-century America in-spired Walter Rauschenbusch to formulate the Social Gospel Movement in response to the desperate plight of the working poor also impelled evangelist Billy Sunday to hit the sawdust trail with his hellfire-and-brimstone message of personal salva-tion. Reading the Bible with others means that we endeavor to understand what each of these radically different individuals can teach us about living out our faith. This requires humility of heart and generosity of spirit—being quick to listen and slow to impose, being ready to learn and reluctant to correct.

Is there any area of community life in which we need to apply the "one anothers" of Scripture as urgently as in the ways in which we interpret and apply the Bible? Inevitably, we will have areas of genuine disagreement, often on serious matters. We have the witness of history and the resources of Church tradition to guide us in clarifying boundaries that are essential to our identity in Christ. But any attempt to bind others to our positions in mat-ters of conscience, cultural sensibilities, Christian practice, and other "gray" areas of Scripture is death-dealing, not life-giving. That is simply not our business. As Paul says, "'All things are lawful,' but not all things build up. Do not seek your own advan-tage, but that of the other" (1 Cor. 10:23–24). This means giving others maximum freedom to follow their own leading by the Spirit, not trying to control them. Our criterion is always, "whether you eat or drink, or whatever you do, do everything for the glory of God" (verse 31).

Micah prophesies the day in which all nations and peoples will stream to the Lord's "house," pitched upon the highest hill in a heaven-on-earth era of peace and security under the Messiah.

Imagine that you are part of the great crowd assembled on "the mountain of the LORD" (4:2), gathered to learn God's ways and walk in God's paths. The People of God have become an all-inclusive, perfectly loving community formed from every tongue and people group of the earth, centered in the Lord of All. Your life experience is just one note of grace among the melodies and chords swirling throughout the assembled throng. Only together will all of you, and each of you, discover the mighty song that the Spirit of God is singing through you.

This is a bit of the glorious reality awaiting us. To get a taste of it now, we need to see and experience life with God through our relational dynamics with others—seeing what they see, understanding what they experience. A balanced vision of life with God will help us read the parts of Scripture in light of the whole of Scripture. It will lead us through the Bible in search of understanding how to plunge our dry lives into the great river of life with God. And just as surely as rivers run toward the sea, this vision will sweep us into the practice of life with God, for we will no longer be satisfied to stand on the banks and watch others swim past.

Moving from vision to practice leads us into the Spiritual Disciplines. They have been called "the means of grace" with good reason—they are the doorway to experiencing the transforming effects of grace in our lives. Each time we cross their threshold, we enter into the great mystery of how the heart of God engages the hearts of people.

Part 3

Understanding the Means

The spirit of the disciplines—that which moves us *to* them and *through* them to prevent them from becoming a new bondage and to deepen constantly, our union with the heart and mind of God—is this love of Jesus, with its steadfast longing and resolute will to be like him.

—Dallas Willard
The Spirit of the Disciplines
(emphasis added)

7

The Disciplines of Relationship

I pray that . . . you may be strengthened in your inner
being with power through his Spirit, and that Christ may
dwell in your hearts through faith, as you are being rooted
and grounded in love.

—Ephesians 3:16–17

On the northwest side of Pikes Peak, the mountain that towers
8,000 feet above Colorado Springs, a highway zigs and zags all the
way to the 14,110-foot summit. If you drive this route and are fortunate to arrive when the mountain is clear—and if you can with-
stand the light-headedness of the sudden altitude change—you will
be greeted with a spectacular view of the "far expanse of mountain
ranges and sea-like sweep of plain" that inspired Katharine Lee
Bates to compose "America the Beautiful."

Now, if you climb the Peak's front face under your own power
along the thirteen miles of rugged Barr trail, when you finally
reach the summit you will feel dizzy not as much from the de-
creased oxygen supply as from the exultation of a hard-won accomplishment. At that moment, if you are privileged to lay eyes
on the dazzling scenery, you may have the curious sense that you

have somehow climbed *into* that vista. You are not outside it looking in, but inside it looking out. That view will become part of you in a way you will never lose. You may even find yourself feeling grateful to the mountain, as if it has allowed you to become an extension of its life, as if you and the Peak have partnered together in this accomplishment.

Life with God is an ongoing, ever-changing, relational adventure. It is not a matter of being driven through life, stopping every now and then to get out of the car and see the surroundings. God invites us to climb into the landscape of our journey, to breathe deeply with full lungs, to feel blood pulsing through muscles doing what they were made to do, to experience the wonder of having a body with which to see and hear and smell and taste and touch this astonishing world.

Do we truly want life with God? This is the prime question in moving from intention to action in the spiritual life. It is not a matter of ability, for "his divine power has given us everything needed for life and godliness, through the knowledge of him who called us by his own glory and goodness" (2 Pet. 1:3).

We have been given "everything needed" because there are things for us to do! God wants an active partner in relationship. The spiritual life is just that—a *life*. We learn as we go. We learn as we do. As we go and do with God, we are changed along the way.

We are called into the struggle and the joy of transformation. We can either pay attention to that call or turn a deaf ear to it. Remember, we are always going *somewhere*. The ancient path of spiritual practice consists of choosing a direction—either to be carried by the drift of the world around us, or to move with the currents of God's love. A Spiritual Discipline is an intentionally directed action, which places us in a position to receive from God the power to do what we cannot accomplish on our own.

This doing and receiving is a Divine-human rhythm of grace-filled interaction—a kind of *"pas de Dieu,"* in which we follow God's lead. The opening step is by divine initiative: "For it is God who is at work in you, enabling you both to will and to work for his good pleasure" (Phil. 2:13). Our human steps in response to the promptings of the Spirit open us to the grace of receiving, for "God will fully satisfy every need of yours according to his riches in glory in Christ Jesus" (Phil. 4:19). God goes ahead of us, God follows us, God holds us up, God is always with us.

THE MEANS TO DEEPER LIFE

As swimming strokes enable the human body to glide smoothly along ocean currents, so the Spiritual Disciplines move us into the transforming rhythms of life with God. Learning to swim entails overcoming the fear of sinking and trusting the reality of the body's buoyancy. Moving into the depths of life with God involves shedding the illusion of self-sufficiency and trusting in God's promise, "I will carry you" (Isa. 46:4).

The deep waters of God's life are already flowing. We simply learn the strokes that will enable us more and more to be at home in them.

Have you ever been to the seashore and felt mesmerized by the rhythms of the waves rising and falling, rising and falling, sometimes crashing ashore, other times gently lapping up onto the sand? The ocean's primal rhythms hold an irresistible fascination for us, whether we are simply walking along the water's edge with waves foaming up around our ankles or just floating on our back, feeling ourselves gently rocked in the bosom of the sea. Despite the imminent sense of danger in its power to rise up in fury and pound us, the ocean's vast strength calls us to become part of it. We hear it in the rhythm of our own blood when we hold a seashell close to our ear. Returning to the ocean feels like finding a way back home again.

In a similar way, "deep calls to deep" (Ps. 42:7) in the rhythms of life with God. There are times when we are caught up in prayer, singing in worship, feeling the goodness of God in the sunshine warming our skin, mentally leaping to a new insight in something we are reading, feeling the bread of God's body pressed into the palm of our hand, when it seems that we are glimpsing the truest life of all. The Spiritual Disciplines give us ways of finding our way home to the heart of God, where we belong.

The Disciplines require us to do things, but not for doing's sake. This doing leads us into being in the presence of God so that we can sense the rhythm of God's heartbeat underlying the surface rhythms of daily life. And being with God is what shapes us, more and more, into the image of God originally planted within us and redeemed in Christ.

We rest in the knowledge that the discipline itself is only a means to deeper life, not the life itself. Let's be clear on what discipline is: the ability to do the right thing at the right time for the right reason. This is not the same as the ability to accomplish the desired result through human effort. God is the One who brings about our inward transformation into Christlikeness.

The human body is our power-pack of mind-body-spirit—we discipline it in order to practice cooperation with God. We have power over what we do with our bodies. We have power over what thoughts we allow to fill our mind. This is the arena of our personal freedom. But we are also spirit, the personal power given to us by God, shaped in God's image, and designed for life in unity and harmony with God. We can indirectly deaden our spirit through actions based on the illusion of our independence from God, but we do not have power to bring it to life. God alone can give life to our spirit, and we can receive that life by staying connected to our Source.

Do you see the difference between what we do, and what God does? We invest our little opportunities for control in turning over ultimate control. We do not have ultimate control anyway— just the illusion of it, at times. We engage in spiritual practices as we choose to do the right thing at the right time for the right reason. God envelops our little practices in sovereign and loving power. That is why we can rest in grace. We do not have direct control over who we become—Christlikeness is a gift of grace. Only God can bring about the progressive transformation of our human spirit into the image of the One who gave us life.

If we find that we are not venturing deeply enough into the waters of life with God, the answer is not to try harder. The answer, simply, is to get rid of more—get rid of our agendas, get rid of our self-concern, get rid of our helplessness and fear, so that we might get more of God. "The Lord is my strength and my song," proclaims Moses (Exod. 15:2, NIV). "The Lord waits to be gracious to you," promises Isaiah (30:18). "Cast all your anxiety on him, because he cares for you," assures Peter (1 Pet. 5:7).

When we say, "God, I will be with You," it is only in response to God's prior declaration, "I am with you." God will meet us at every step, leading us to the place of holy change. This is why the Spiritual Disciplines are not the same as "holy habits." They may be habitual practices, but in and of themselves they have no power to make us righteous or holy. They are morally and spiritually neutral, for they can be exercised either in self-seeking or in God-seeking. God seeks to do an inward work in our lives, but it will not be forced upon us. Spiritual practice is simply a way for us to position ourselves so that Christ can dwell within us. "Draw near to God, and he will draw near to you," James tells us (4:8).

A helpful image for understanding practice of the Disciplines is to envision a path along a narrow mountaintop ridge, with drop-offs on either side. This is the path of "disciplined grace"— disciplined because there are choices for us to make; grace because the outcome of our choices is secured by the love of God. This path leads to the deep change and renewal for which we long. On either side of this path are the distortions of discipline to which we fall prey when we separate them from the context of relationship.

On one side, we so elevate discipline that it becomes an end rather than the means. Forgetting that our actions are invited and supported and sustained by grace, we lose sight of God and focus on human performance. The Pharisees and Sadducees did this in their obsession with rule keeping and performance. We do this today when we judge one another according to our own ideas of external righteousness—a form of legalism that ignores the attitude of the heart and has nothing to do with the righteousness of Jesus. This inflated view of discipline is a form of moralism, which reduces relationship by squeezing God out of it, leaving only human performance. Any time we feel pride in our own practice of the Disciplines, or try to gauge whether others are practicing them, we are on the slippery slope of this chasm.

On the other side of the path of disciplined grace lies a drop-off into what Dietrich Bonhoeffer calls "cheap grace." At the opposite extreme of legalism, this view devalues discipline. Sometimes called *antinomianism* (from the Greek for "against" and "law"), it reasons that since we cannot earn righteousness, we receive grace freely without accountability to the requirements of the law. But as Bonhoeffer observed, although grace is free, that does not mean it is cheap. Grace requires something of us in order to do its transforming work in our lives. God does not bestow it upon us automatically. God invites us to experience it.

We are always being formed by *something*. If we remain passive, we are being formed in the likeness of our surrounding environment. That thought alone should give us pause before dismissing the importance of disciplined effort.

Again, it is not the effort of walking the path of disciplined grace that produces the change. But that effort is what positions us to receive the gracious work of God in forming, reforming, and transforming us. As a direct result of the work of God strengthening us in our inner being, the holy habits of the Christian life take shape within us: love, joy, peace, patience, kindness, generosity, faithfulness, gentleness, and self-control.

The fruit of the Spirit is the outward evidence of the inward reality of the heart. We practice the Disciplines in order to be fully present to God, not in order to try harder to bear spiritual fruit. These habits of holiness are the fruit of Christ's life in us, a work of God's Spirit in our lives. As we pursue life with God, they will gradually permeate our lives, and we will begin habitually to reflect the character of Christ.

JESUS IS THE LIFE

Sometimes we approach the topic of spiritual practice with a sense of weariness, as if we have to try harder again at something we have already failed at doing. Frustration is natural, but there is no reason why we should have to accept it as the norm. As with any area of life, frustration can crop up for a variety of reasons: genuine fatigue, a self-imposed sense of all-or-nothing, real or assumed obstacles that need resolving. In the area of spiritual practice, it is a common mistake to assume that if we will only do "enough" spiritual practice, our efforts will result in a satisfying spiritual life.

This is a subtle but highly effective temptation because it contains a grain of truth—wrapped, of course, in a great many layers of distortion. The truth is that spiritual practice, bathed in desire for God, will take us more deeply into life with God. One of the distortions encasing it is that it is up to us to "get" a life with God.

The testimony of the Scripture is that *God* has already gotten a life for us in Christ. We need only participate in the life already offered to us. We may rest with relief and freedom in the knowledge that it is not up to us to create a spiritual life through spiritual practices. That would be like asking a child to create her own family life by amassing enough childlike actions to make it come true. In a healthy family, there is already a life established by loving parents, who joyfully bring the child into their family. It is not the child's place to take on the roles of the parents in creating that life.

Our heavenly Father has given us his Son so that we might know and participate in the kingdom life God has already created. When Jesus came announcing the kingdom, he was declaring its accessibility to us through him. The Spiritual Disciplines train us for life in the kingdom. But Jesus himself is the "way, and the truth, and the life" (John 14:6). Paul tells us, "your life is hidden with Christ" (Col. 3:3). This life has been flowing since the beginning in the *Logos,* God's Word. It is full of grace and truth. It shines eternal light through every dark place in the human soul, through every particle of dark matter in the universe. It has taken on flesh and dwelt among us, so that we might see this Word for ourselves, and believe, and turn from our darkness into the light. With the saving grace given to us before the beginning of time (2 Tim. 1:9), we find our true home and become our true self in the Word made flesh, who holds this eternal life in trust for us, hidden in the marvelous depths of his being.

This miracle of a life "hidden in Christ" is a real, lived experience, not just a belief about our eternal destiny. It is not just conjecture about a mystical reality. It is not just for the hereafter, but for the here-and-now. Jesus uses the image of himself as the true Vine and his followers as the branches to teach us that spiritual fruit grows from him, not from our self-effort (see John 15:1–7). When he says that we should abide in him, he really means it.

This is not just a pretty metaphor or a clever idea—it is an actual way of living.

OUR MEANS OF PURSUING LIFE WITH GOD

What are the Spiritual Disciplines? Well, simply, they are practices for pursuing life with God drawn from the teaching of Scripture and illuminated in the lives of those who practice them. There is no exhaustive list, but there is a range of core Disciplines that have been recognized throughout history to be helpful in nurturing the soul.

Now there are many different ways of understanding and categorizing the Disciplines. What is important are not the boundaries of such categories but what they reveal about the role of the Disciplines in our lives. Each way of approaching them suggests unique insights into the role of the Disciplines in our life with God. Think of the differing views of the Disciplines as facets through which to view the same jewel: the reality of the means of grace provided for our life with God.

A classic way of organizing the Disciplines is through the categories of abstinence and engagement, as Dallas Willard uses in his seminal study *The Spirit of the Disciplines*. Generally speaking, Disciplines of abstinence—solitude, silence, fasting, frugality, chastity, secrecy, and sacrifice—counteract tendencies toward sins of commission, following Peter's instruction to "abstain from the desires of the flesh that wage war against the soul" (1 Pet. 2:11). However, this does not mean that the desires we discipline through abstinence are themselves wrong. Rather, by interludes of refraining from satisfying our natural needs for food, sexual expression, companionship, leisure enjoyment, and so forth, we help curb these impulses. The Disciplines of abstinence allow us to bring all human desires under the grace of God. We put up guardrails so that these good gifts do not overrun healthy boundaries and become unhealthy obsessions. In addition to channeling our natural desires so they do not overwhelm us, practicing abstinence also carves out room in our lives for active pursuit of the ways of the kingdom.

Through the Disciplines of engagement, we are called to what we might otherwise neglect through sins of omission. We retrain our sin-distorted ideas of what is good and right by plunging ourselves in activity that the world often disdains. Through study, worship, celebration, service, prayer, fellowship, confession, and submission, we learn what is truly life-giving. Where sin has twisted our understanding, engagement corrects it. Where failure has sent us into hiding, engagement calls us forth. Where experience has robbed us of trust in God, engagement helps us find it again so that we can exclaim with the psalmist, "Bless the LORD, O my soul, and do not forget all his benefits" (103:2).

The core Disciplines are at the heart of Christian practice because they directly position us to receive the flow of God's life through us. We can see the centrality of fasting and prayer, for example, in Luke's portrayal of the prophet Anna, who is widowed early in her marriage and spends the rest of her life at the Temple, praying and fasting "night and day" (Luke 2:37). We know nothing about her life except for her role in the climactic event of the presentation of the infant Jesus at the Temple.

This is the event featuring the great *Nunc Dimittis* of Simeon, a man whose whole life has been dedicated to waiting upon the

Lord for the "consolation of Israel," now arrived in the flesh in the form of the baby he takes into his arms. Simeon praises God for "your salvation, which you have prepared in the presence of all peoples, a light for revelation to the Gentiles and for glory to your people Israel" (Luke 2:30–32). He also prophesies foreboding news to Mary: "This child is destined for the falling and the rising of many in Israel, and to be a sign that will be opposed so that the inner thoughts of many will be revealed—and a sword will pierce your own soul too" (2:34).

Now is the moment when Anna, whose life to this point remains obscure to us, steps forth onto the stage of redemption. Perhaps all her years of giving herself to God in body and mind and spirit have prepared her to recognize the Christ child. We don't know that with certainty, but we do know that the woman who has spent a lifetime being with God is now the one who proclaims the reality of God with us: "At that moment she came, and began to praise God and to speak about the child to all who were looking for the redemption of Jerusalem" (2:38).

We can see in Anna a beautiful harmony of inner life and outer testimony. We can also see the striking juxtaposition of a life steeped in solitude—and no doubt loneliness—and a life that becomes critically important to the community of God's people. Anna's outsider status as a widow is radically reversed to an insider role in redemption history.

Our ideas of importance are so vastly different than God's priorities that we never know what God may be preparing for us in our day-to-day acts of trust. This is a crucial function of the Disciplines—to prepare us in "little" ways for the "big" work God is doing in our lives.

Notice that in Simeon's prophecy about Jesus, he declares the child will become the occasion of revealing the "inner thoughts" of many. Here again is one of the great themes of Scripture, that God "looks upon the heart" (see 1 Sam. 16:7, for example). The heart has been called "the seat of the soul" because above all other organs, it is the center of our most vital life function: literally, it pumps the lifeblood through our veins. We are learning much about how to tend to the physical health of the heart, but we are also learning that where the heart is concerned, spiritual health cannot be separated from physical health. The human person is a mysterious unity of mind, body, and spirit. From a scriptural standpoint, the health of the spirit is fundamental to the health of the whole person. Therefore, says the writer of Proverbs, "Keep your heart with all vigilance, for from it flow the springs of life" (4:23).

Another way of understanding the classic Disciplines, in addition to the rhythms of abstinence and engagement, is through the lens of the unity of the human person. Disciplines shaping our inward life—meditation, prayer, fasting, and study—build a strong foundation for our outward life. But character is formed through action, as well, and therefore we practice the Disciplines of the outward life—simplicity, solitude, submission, and service. Character is revealed through behavior, but behavior influences and shapes character.

The core Disciplines also give us a rhythm of life alone, and life together. Our spiritual formation takes place individually, person by person, but also in community. Life in Christ is a wondrous integration of individual personhood extending into eternity, and the unity of all persons in the eternal, beloved community centered in Christ. Therefore, we practice corporate Disciplines—confession, worship, guidance, and celebration. These are means of practicing life together as the People of God, all of them instituted by God for our health and well-being.

An immediate difficulty presents itself, however, as soon as we "define" the Disciplines. Our tendency is to create an official way of identifying and arranging them, so that we have a sense of mastery over them. If we know "all" the Disciplines, and we can track the ways in which we practice them, then we can feel as if we are "succeeding" at life with God. This is precisely the trap that the leaders of the Law fell into in Jesus' day. They kept track—privately and publicly—of how well they fulfilled the commandments. They were constantly on the lookout to catch others who were breaking them or failing to fulfill them. That gave them a false sense of superiority. "Woe to you ... hypocrites," Jesus said to these religious professionals. "For you are like whitewashed tombs ... on the outside [you] look righteous to others, but inside you are full of hypocrisy and lawlessness" (Matt. 23:27–28).

We can have a clear understanding of the spiritual practices instituted by God and verified by the People of God. But we do not have a set of rules! This gives us a wondrous freedom in life with God, for whatever leads to the hardening of our spirit is no longer a "spiritual" discipline, but a human-only discipline, done without God. And conversely, whatever leads to the genuine formation of our spirit in Christlikeness can become for us a "spiritual" discipline: walking in the woods; singing and making music; creating a work of art; laughing with friends in the goodness of companionship; caring for animals; or, like Brother

Lawrence, performing simple tasks associated with meeting food and shelter needs for self and others.

I remember being at Fuller Theological Seminary and watching then-President David Hubbard in his regular practice of leaving the office early to head down to Chavez Ravine (now Dodger Stadium) and watch the Los Angeles Dodgers play. He'd get there in time to see them go through warm-up exercises and the first few innings of play, and then he would leave. We who find ourselves constantly running in overdrive would be well advised to take his example under consideration and make "play" a Spiritual Discipline. Are you so conformed to the demands upon your time and attention that it is hindering your life with God? Go watch a baseball game!

THE LIBERTY OF THE DISCIPLINES

"For freedom Christ has set us free," declares Paul. "Stand firm, therefore, and do not submit again to a yoke of slavery" (Gal. 5:1). Paul is countering a kind of slavery that is very religious: an attempt to work hard to gain God's approval instead of living obediently in response to the joyful freedom of God's grace. This is precisely the kind of slavery we inflict on one another when we attempt to define and manage and enforce any mode or habit of practicing the presence of God. That is the way of legalism, which is the way of death to the spirit.

In the next chapter we will explore more specifically how the Disciplines actually work, and why they are always and only a means to life, not Life itself. This is just as true of how we practice reading the Bible as it is of how we practice fasting and study, or service and worship. Any time we make spiritual practice our central focus, rather than life with God, we are creating a rigid system. Rigid systems destroy life. The *Disciplines* of relationship always serve the *dynamics* of relationship. When they are detached from those dynamics, then we know we are in need of a fresh infusion of grace.

The good news is that such transformation is always available to us. God is always ready and willing to take what we can do in order to accomplish within us what we cannot do on our own. The God who is "rich in mercy" has given us life in Jesus, so that not only in the ages to come, but also in the life we live today, "he might show the immeasurable riches of his grace in kindness toward us in Christ Jesus" (Eph. 2:4, 7). The Spiritual Disciplines are the doorway to freedom in God's work, not our own: "For by grace you have been saved through faith, and this is not your own doing; it is the gift of God—not the result of works, so that no one may boast. For we are what he has made us, created in Christ Jesus for good works, which God prepared beforehand to be our way of life" (Eph. 2:8–10). What a glorious and grace-filled partnership!

8

The Way of Freedom

But those who look into the perfect law, the law of liberty, and persevere, being not hearers who forget but doers who act—they will be blessed in their doing.

—James 1:25

In this day of fractious religious arguments, we could do with less debate over who may be counted among the faithful and more evidence of faithful witness to the way of Christ. We might open floodgates of healing and redemption were we to lay down our arguments and engage every aspect of life in answering God's gracious invitation, "I am with you—will you be with Me?"

The quiet power of a life transformed by the grace of God is so explosive that it can redirect the course of human events. Consider the story of John Woolman, a successful tradesman in colonial America who pared down his business in order to live simply and fully in response to the pull of divine Grace upon his life.

Raised on a farm in a modest Jersey village, Woolman had an unusually sensitive spirit early in life, keenly attuned to the rhythms of the Divine Spirit. Although he struggled anxiously with the temptations and wantonness of youth, he was constantly aware of "the operations of Divine Love" within his own heart. His spiritual understanding was charged with awareness of God's tender mercy and love for all living creatures. So perhaps it was no surprise that in his itinerant Quaker ministry, he became a gracious yet tireless and uncompromising advocate for concerns such as the abolition of slavery, just relations with Native Americans, an end to taxation in support of war, and refusal to benefit from consumer goods produced by slave labor and unjust trade practices.

In his classic *Journal,* Woolman reveals the ways in which he steadily cultivated a gentle receptiveness to "Divine Breathings" that forged his convictions and naturally led him to take a stand on them in every aspect of his life. For a wondrous picture of how the Spiritual Disciplines help reshape all of life around the divine Center, I recommend undertaking an acquaintance with Woolman through his writings. To whet your appetite, I will tell you just one story from his life.

As background to understanding the significance of this incident, it is important to know that Woolman's convictions about the evils of slavery grew over time, as again and again he was "afflicted in mind" by this debasing treatment of fellow human beings. His *Journal* indicates that during this time he was spending many hours in prayer and fasting, periods of solitude and silence, meditation upon the Scripture, service, simplicity of lifestyle and speech, worship with others, and outdoor study of God's tender love for all living creatures.

Our story finds John one November evening in 1758, being hosted in the home of Thomas Woodward after preaching powerfully against slavery at a Quaker meeting. Please be aware that at this point Woolman has earned a reputation as a gracious man, not given to sharing his opinions unless he feels divinely compelled to do so. And when he does speak, it is always quietly and respectfully, never confrontationally. Because of his humble and loving manner, he exerts an unusually powerful influence upon others.

When John enters the Woodward home, undoubtedly tired and hungry, he notices servants and inquires as to their status. When he learns they are slaves, he says not a word. Later that night, however, he quietly gets out of bed, writes a note to his host explaining why he cannot receive their hospitality, goes to the slaves' quarters and pays them for the day's service, and walks out into the night. His silent testimony pierces conventional attitudes and behavior like a carefully aimed arrow of the Spirit. When the household stirs to life the following morning, Thomas Woodward—over his wife's vehement protests—sets free all his slaves. One more Friend has joined the abolitionist movement.

There are many such remarkable stories in Woolman's living testimony against the inhumanity of slave owning. Collectively, they form a wedge applying steady pressure against the practice of slavery—first among Woolman's own denomination, the Quakers, and ultimately throughout the Western world.

I hope this little account gives you a glimpse of what can happen when we are faithful to be "doers" of the Word, not just hearers. But make no mistake: we are doers of the Word, not doers of the supernatural work of the Word implanted in our hearts. Much heartache and grievous error results from mistakenly equating these two in our lives. John Woolman did not rise up one day and declare, "I shall be a mighty force for God against the slave trade!" and then plot a ministry plan to implement his strategic objective. No, he simply and humbly attended to Divine Breathings in the variety of means that were available to him. That is why when the moment came for him to speak, or to act, he was already prepared to do so.

Think of Woolman's evening at the Woodward home. As a naturally shy and unassuming man, it would have been unnatural for Woolman to behave as he did. Abolitionist convictions had not yet spread among the Quakers, so having slaves did not seem cruel or out of the ordinary to most people—hard as that is for us to understand today. We can, however, understand the social pressure of convention, of blending in with the crowd. Woolman was the kind of person who shrinks from giving offense to others, especially in a way that could appear to pass judgment upon them. What gave him the strength to act against his own natural inclinations? What changed his natural inclinations into "unnatural" tendencies?

I will tell you what gave him the strength: life with God. His steady strokes of swimming in the deep waters of God's mercy and love re-formed his natural inclinations. As his spiritual practices opened him to ever-deepening levels of transformation through the Holy Spirit, it became unnatural for him to act in ordinary human ways.

It would be silly to expect that in his own effort, Woolman could devise and then carry out a series of action steps for his strategic ministry plan that would lead to the powerful witness God gave him. His self-consciousness alone would have stopped him from imagining himself the hero, and his sensitivity would undoubtedly have had him second-guessing himself at every turn. *Let's see, if I eat meat served by slaves in the Woodward home, does it fall under Paul's permission to eat meat offered to idols? After all, I have just preached for the Lord. Surely He wants me to have sustenance and strength for tomorrow's demands in my important ministry for him. And Paul does command slaves to be respectful to their owners. On the other hand, I know it is wrong for me to enjoy God's good gifts when my fellow humans are deprived of them and must serve them to me at the expense of their own freedom and dignity.* Such deliberations might have paralyzed him into inaction.

Do you remember our definition of *discipline? The ability to do the right thing at the right time for the right reason.* This takes prior preparation. Dallas Willard observes that this is the kind of unthinking readiness Jesus has in mind when he advises us not to let the right hand know what the left hand is doing. It is what heart surgeon Dr. William C. DeVries had in mind when he described practicing multiple times the implantation of an artificial heart in animals. He wanted to be ready for the moment when he installed the first artificial heart in a human being. "The reason you practice so much," he explained, "is so that you will do things automatically the same way every time."[25]

The bottom-line goal of practicing the Spiritual Disciplines is so that when the moment of action comes, our automatic default-mode is to "act naturally" according to the Spirit, not the flesh, as Paul describes in such marvelous detail in chapters 6 through 8 of his letter to the Romans. But of course, what "acting naturally" looks like depends on whether we are still "slaves of sin" or "slaves of righteousness" (Rom. 6:17–18). To help us understand the difference between these two conditions, Paul uses an agricultural metaphor in his epistle to the Galatians: "If you sow to your own flesh, you will reap corruption from the flesh; but if you sow to the Spirit, you will reap eternal life from the Spirit" (6:8). In growing grain, farmers do what they can—preparing the soil, planting the seeds, watering, protecting from predators—and then wait on what they do not control (weather, supply and demand, environmental factors) while the seasons of growth take place. We do things that are within our volition and power to do. Over time and space, growth in our character takes place. In time, inward character shapes outward behavior, and the cycles of transformation continue by grace.

What it looks like when we are steadily being transformed into the likeness of Christ is John Woolman's quiet reaction to the slaves in the Woodward home. It is turning the other cheek instead of reacting in kind when someone attacks our character. It is responding in forbearance instead of anger when we put on our turn signal and another car speeds up to cut us off before we can change lanes. It is breathing a silent prayer instead of lashing back when a loved one says something hurtful.

The goal of practicing the Spiritual Disciplines is not to do more of them. Rather, it is to incorporate them into our lives at the right time in the right way for the right reason. As Dallas Willard explains, Jesus' mastery of life in the spirit shows us that "spiritual strength is not manifested by great and extensive practice of the spiritual Disciplines, *but by little need to practice them and still maintain full spiritual life.*"[26]

THE PRINCIPLE OF INDIRECTION

John Woolman's life illuminates for us a liberating truth: *we do not become godly by trying to become godly*. We become godly as "holy habits" such as love, joy, and peace fill our character so that we do the right thing at the right time with the right motive, instinctively . . . without thinking about it. Woolman knew instinctively that slavery was wrong because he had developed a keen attentiveness to God's loving care for every living thing, animal as well as human.

Through his spiritual practices, Woolman steeped himself in the Presence of Divine Love and thus became increasingly familiar with its "operations" . . . living in relationship to Divine Love, he increasingly took on its character . . . and increasingly formed by that character, he instinctively responded in ways that reflected Divine Love. He made decisions based upon what he learned through relating with God. This inward formation led him, increasingly, to act against the common positions of his time—initially by prompting from uneasiness and lack of clearness, then by growing convictions, and ultimately to a full-blown understanding of the social evils of his day.

Woolman is a magnificent illustration of the principle of indirection. Indirection affirms that *spiritual formation does not occur by direct human effort, but through a relational process whereby we receive from God the power or ability to do what we cannot do by our own effort*. We do not produce the outcome. That is God's business. We enter into an interactive relational life with God utilizing appropriate Disciplines for the training of body, mind, and spirit in righteousness. The result of all of that is a character formation that is in excess of anything we could have hoped or dreamed—a life filled with righteousness, peace, and joy in the Holy Spirit.

The reason the Spiritual Disciplines do not make us spiritual is because there is nothing inherently spiritual in them. We do not acquire godliness the way bodybuilders build muscle in a solitary regimen. We pray in order to engage in relationship, not to count how many minutes we spend as if tracking the number of repetitions in a set or the number of sets in a workout. We immerse ourselves in Scripture to engage with the living Word, not to measure our biblical knowledge the way weight lifters monitor how many pounds they can bench press.

We do not produce change by practicing the Disciplines—we receive it. Spiritual growth is a gift, not an accomplishment. This is why Paul explains to an immature Corinthian flock caught up in power struggles over its spiritual shepherd:

> For when one says, "I belong to Paul," and another, "I belong to Apollos," are you not merely human? What then is Apollos? What is Paul? Servants through whom you came to believe, as the LORD assigned to each. I planted, Apollos watered, but God gave the growth. So neither the one who plants nor the one who waters is anything, but only God who gives the growth. (1 Cor. 3:4–7)

Instead of taking on responsibility for our growth directly, we do it on the slant. Rather than trying to overcome pride by attacking our reasons for feeling proud, we undertake Disciplines of service. Over time, these actions put us in a proper relationship with others, which brings humility . . . hence overcoming pride. If gossip or empty talk is a struggle, we train through silence. If greed, we retrain our view of possessing things by engaging in simplicity, frugality, giving. If cursing, we train by blessing those who provoke our anger, taking up the habit of blessing for a month or so until we are more apt to bless than to curse.

We address vices by attending to the opposite virtues, and then seeking which Disciplines will train us in those virtues. Virtues are the good habits we can rely on to make our lives work. Vices are the bad habits we can rely on—just as surely—to make our lives not work (dysfunctional). As we place ourselves before God with various Disciplines, we can be filled with more of God's life as we are baptized into the milieu of the Holy Spirit. The mind conforms to the order of what it concentrates upon. The heart conforms to the beauty of what it gazes upon. As they are re-formed, we take on more of Christ's likeness. Vices will naturally diminish and virtues increase.

I want to share with you some practical guidelines drawn from Scripture that will lead us by the process of indirection into the way of "the law of liberty" with the Disciplines. These guidelines are guardrails to keep us from veering off into the way of law—bondage to self-effort. We enter the life of the kingdom of God by receiving it as a gift, not by trying to enter the life of the kingdom. Still, there are things for us to do that prepare heart and mind so that we might become adequate vessels for receiving God's grace. In this circumstance, the form that grace takes is the ongoing character transformation—new attitudes, new spirit, a more loving heart.

TRAINING, NOT TRYING HARDER

Paul uses the metaphor of an athlete in training to illustrate the path of spiritual maturity:

> Do you not know that in a race the runners all compete, but only one receives the prize? Run in such a way that you may win it. Athletes exercise self-control in all things; they do it to receive a perishable wreath, but we an imperishable one. So I do not run aimlessly, nor do I box as though beating the air; but I punish my body and enslave it, so that after proclaiming to others I myself should not be disqualified. (1 Cor. 9:24–27)

This kind of training is not about earthly goals of winning or losing. It prepares us for life in the all-inclusive community of Love by enabling us to receive more of God's life and power, that we might be more capable of acting in love.

Training is necessary preparation for doing the right thing at the right time for the right reason. But this is not the same thing as trying harder.

Much of our frustration in life arises from worrying about or trying to manage things that are simply beyond our direct control—who gets promoted at work; if a relationship is all we want it to be; whether the car breaks down or the rent goes up; a family member's choices that have consequences on us. It is difficult to let go of trying to make things turn out the way we want them to.

So it is in our life with God. Determined to have a deeper spiritual life, we think we have to try harder. But a far better goal than trying harder is training. This is the training we do in the life of the kingdom of God as the athletes of God. The metaphor breaks down in that an athlete training gets a result equal to the training put in. In the spiritual life we are training with a supernatural Partner. The results are always far in excess of the work put in—this is the sign of the work of the Spirit upon us. Little training . . . much larger results.

What does this mean, in practical terms? Say we are having difficulty in the area of sexual temptation. Sexuality is an enormously powerful and fundamental dimension of being human, and I do not mean to reduce it to channeling urges. For our purposes here, however, I will simply focus on those everyday choices we make within the particular contexts, opportunities, and challenges unique to our individual lives and sexual experience.

Without prior preparation, trying harder to restrain sexual expression by mustering willpower at the brink of temptation is nearly akin to attempting to hold an inflatable beach ball underwater. That is repression, which will simply come back at us from another angle, trapping us in a cycle of failure, self-punishment, and anger. Indirection establishes a pattern of disciplining the body's desires long before we face the moment of decision. Our human cravings and desires are like rivers—if not properly channeled, they tend to overflow their banks. The original monastic idea of chastity did not primarily focus on sexual sin, but on the right control of desire. "Chastity" meant the right control of all desires by the grace of God. This is where fasting is helpful, because it dethrones the body as master and gives us authority over our body. We learn that cravings need not control us.

A practical result of indirection is that discipline in one area often produces results in several areas, as twelve-step programs designed to help alcohol addicts prove useful for other destructive behavior patterns. The benefits of fasting extend to many areas of impulse control: pornography addiction, food cravings, Internet obsessions, or everyday activities such as shopping or television watching used to excess. The Spiritual Discipline of fasting teaches us not to repress desire, but to rechannel it properly.

We do not produce the change; we receive it. This is why fasting must forever center on God. If we allow ourselves to take pride in accomplishing it, it serves false religion, not true. When Jesus gives instructions about fasting (Matt. 6:16–18), he focuses not on technique or results but on our motives for doing so. When fasting is properly combined with worship—as we see in the prophetess Anna (Luke 2:37) and the apostolic band at Antioch (Acts 13:2)—it is a wonderful practice for hollowing out sacred space in which to focus on the sufficiency of and goodness of God to meet all our needs. Fasting is feasting on God.

CULTIVATING A HOLY EXPECTANCY

This focus provides a second guardrail in the principle of indirection: cultivating a holy expectancy that God will act in and through our efforts to do what we can do. Becoming "doers" of the Word according to the "perfect law of liberty" means that God brings about the transformation we seek. As we take steps to cooperate with the work of the Divine in our lives, the Spirit will do within us what we are powerless to do. As Paul encourages us, "I am confident of this, that the one who began a good work among you will bring it to completion by the day of Jesus Christ" (Phil. 1:6).

Two utterly unquestioned values in our culture today are desire and freedom—to put it bluntly, "I do what I want, when I want, to the extent that I want." The cultural idol of the self has distorted our understanding of freedom in Christ so that too often it is reduced to license, or cheap grace. Yet self-seeking ultimately leaves us empty, for the gratification is fleeting and shallow. It drains us instead of filling us, leaving us in greater need than we were before.

But on the other side of license lies moralism. Indirection reminds us that we are not in control, God is. It is tempting to think that with spiritual practice we are earning a life with God—but this is the way of self-effort. The way of Christ is receiving the life that only God can give us. The Spiritual Disciplines are always and only the means to participating in this life, not a ladder to climb up to attain it.

This is why the prophet Isaiah calls out:

Ho, everyone who thirsts,
come to the waters;
and you that have no money,
come, buy and eat!
Come, buy wine and milk
without money and without price.
Why do you spend your money for that which is not bread,
and your labor for that which does not satisfy? (55:1–2)

If we are willing to learn patiently and slowly about our needs, then the Scripture will help us learn to rely on Divine provision for them. Yes, there is something for us to do. But we do not need to purchase this provision with our efforts on the path of disciplined grace. That is the way of Law, the way of the scribes and Pharisees: "They tie up heavy burdens, hard to bear, and lay them on the shoulders of others; but they themselves are unwilling to lift a finger to move them" (Matt. 23:4).

The provision is already ours. We need not grasp feverishly for it like impatient and fretful children oblivious to the calming voice of a loving parent waiting to help them. Jesus has promised to be our ever-present Teacher and Guide. His direction is not beyond our understanding. His voice is not beyond the range of our hearing. If we are willing to listen to the Wonderful Counselor, we will receive the counsel we need.

The Bible introduces us to the concept of holy expectancy in the worship of the People of God. From Moses entering the Tabernacle to the psalmists in procession to the early Church in Acts, they gathered in confidence that they would hear the *Kol Yahweh,* the voice of God. This same assurance is ours as we take humble steps into the with God life. As the writer to the Hebrews declares: "We have this hope, a sure and steadfast anchor of the soul, a hope that enters the inner shrine behind the curtain, where Jesus, a forerunner on our behalf, has entered . . ." (6:19–20).

The spiritual life is not overshadowed by fear or anxiety. It is grounded in the trustworthiness of God's character and the revelation of God in Jesus, the "great high priest" who has brought us into the very holiest place where God dwells, that we might be there together with him. This is not only our confidence in God being *with* us, it is also our guarantee that God understands what it is like to be a human being, making our way through a world that is constantly pulling us in other directions. For "we do not have a high priest who is unable to sympathize with our weaknesses, but we have one who in every respect has been tested as we are, yet without sin. Let us therefore approach the throne of grace with boldness, so that we may receive mercy and find grace to help in time of need" (Heb. 4:15–16).

Are we fearful that God will not provide for our material needs? Then we can practice the corresponding freedom, giving, with trust that God will confirm the promise: "And my God will fully satisfy every need of yours according to his riches in glory in Christ Jesus" (Phil. 4:19).

Are we anxious about how others see us, whether we are valuable to them? Then we can practice the Discipline of solitude with the holy expectancy of the psalmist: "For God alone my soul waits in silence, for my hope is from him" (62:5).

Cultivating a holy expectancy will keep us attuned to the Divine Breathings in our everyday life. If we are veering off the path of disciplined grace, the gentle whisper of the Spirit will call us back. Even the most "spiritual" of activities can turn a Discipline of grace into a self-seeking preoccupation. In *The Sacrament of the Present Moment,* Jean-Pierre De Caussade advises that if the duty of the present moment is to read your Bible, then do it. But if the Spirit is leading you in the present moment to go fix supper for the community and you stay in your room reading the Bible, that is sin.

We practice the Disciplines not for ourselves, but for God, with God, expecting the true bread that satisfies our souls. When we do not turn them into the way of rules and self-effort, which leads to anxiety and bondage, they free us to trust wholly in God. This is the liberty of the Disciplines.

Holy Obedience follows on the heels of Holy Expectancy. What we are asked to do we are given the power to do.

FROM SELF-EFFORT TO SEEKING THE KINGDOM

In addition to the first two guardrails of indirection, "training, not trying harder" and "cultivating a holy expectancy," a third is "from self-effort to seeking the kingdom."

Americans live in a consumer culture unprecedented in its gross excess. We have an embarrassing array of choices for everything, from toothpaste to television, foodstuffs to furniture. Under constant pressure to buy more, we fill our households and then spill over into storage rental units. Despite the trends of recent decades toward simple living and reduced consumption, we have not been slowing in our consumption of "stuff."

"Do not store up for yourselves treasures on earth, where moth and rust consume and where thieves break in and steal; but store up for yourselves treasures in heaven. . . . For where your treasure is, there your heart will be also," Jesus says (Matt. 6:19–21).

The Disciplines reorient us for life in the kingdom of God by retraining our habits, our thoughts and attitudes, and our behavior according to a radically different way of life from what passes for "normal" in this world. Therefore, Jesus says, "Strive first for the kingdom of God and his righteousness, and all these things will be given to you as well" (Matt. 6:33). The "all these things" to which he refers are basic creaturely needs for food, water, clothing, and shelter.

Pause for a moment and consider how much time, money, energy, and thought you spend on meeting these basic needs for yourself, for family members (and pets), for friends and visitors in your home. All of it is fertile ground for learning the ways of life with God.

When Jesus tells us to consider how God provides for the birds of the air and the lilies of the field, he is giving us not license to be irresponsible in what we can control, but freedom to trust God for all things: what is given us to control, and the givens that are beyond our control—family conflicts, natural disasters, business closings, health crises, rising costs of rents and mortgages, economic changes. In the kingdom of this world, these variables keep us anxious and preoccupied. Paul models for us the radical reversal of such conditions in the kingdom of God: "I have learned to be content with whatever I have. I know what it is to have little, and I know what it is to have plenty. . . . I have learned the secret of being well-fed and of going hungry, of having plenty and of being in need" (Phil. 4:11–12).

By indirection, as we practice the Disciplines we learn to handle the things of this world—body, mind, spirit, time, possessions, relationships, work, nature—according to the values of the kingdom, not the values of this world. We are storing up treasure in heaven.

How easy it is to clutch the things of this world and measure our contentment on what is within our grasp. This is the anxious, me-first way of self-effort—*if I work hard enough to achieve the good life, I deserve whatever I can get for myself.* But Jesus says:

Come to me, all you that are weary and are carrying heavy burdens, and I will give you rest. Take my yoke upon you, and learn from me; for I am gentle and humble in heart, and you will find rest for your souls. For my yoke is easy, and my burden is light. (Matt. 11:28–29)

The way of the kingdom sets our feet on the path of freedom. It is impossible to take on the light yoke of Jesus if we are already strapped into the weighty harness of self-effort and willpower.

One Discipline that I have found especially helpful for learning how to take on the easy yoke is studying the lives of those who blaze the trail ahead of us on the path of disciplined grace. When I was fresh out of seminary in my first church pastorate, I encountered deeply needy people—and quickly discovered that I was one of them. They were parched for the living water of spiritual substance. But when I tried to lead them to it by enthusiasm and self-effort, I found that my own resources quickly ran dry. I needed help in moving to a deeper level of life with God, for myself and for our faith community.

I turned in earnest to Devotional Masters of the Christian faith—Augustine; Saint Francis; Julian of Norwich; Teresa of Avila; Brother Lawrence; A. W. Tozer; and many others. After my initial acquaintance with them in my academic coursework, I now wanted to know far more about how they walked through this world so deeply immersed in a life rich in God. What ignited their burning vision for the fire of God at the center of their lives? How did they keep their inner flame so white-hot that it cut a purifying swath through the underbrush of human deception and brokenness?

I found great relief for my dry soul by soaking in the stories of these astounding men and women. Their lives were utterly transformed by their intimate awareness of God in every minute and every circumstance of their lives. Here was a path into life in the kingdom such as I had never experienced or even dreamed possible. I began to desire this kind of life for myself—and with the desire came seeking, and with the seeking came finding. What I found settled me and deepened me, redirecting the course of my ministry and my life. Those experiences led me into the Spiritual Disciplines with a momentum that eventually pushed me into writing my first book on the topic.

We let go of self-effort in practicing the Disciplines, and we discover the grace of God's work within us. Then the Disciplines reorient our lives toward seeking the kingdom instead of living on the dry husks of self-effort, and we find that it becomes more natural to live *with* God than to live without God. That is when we begin to understand a fourth benefit of indirection—traveling light.

TRAVELING LIGHT

Here is a desperately needed grace for all those who are earnest about the Spiritual Disciplines: freedom from taking ourselves too seriously. It is an occupational hazard of devout folk to become stuffy bores. This should not be. After all, Jesus was accused of being a partygoer, eating and drinking with disreputable men and women. Many of us are so circumspect we could not even aspire to such accusations.

Paul cautions us not to think more highly of ourselves than we ought to think (Rom. 12:3). We can also avoid thinking of ourselves more *often* than we ought to think. The guideline of traveling light is a guard against the besetting sin of being overly interested in our own piety.

The Discipline of celebration is a bracing antidote to religious solemnity. It loosens our grip on self-consciousness and brings us back down to earth on the level playing field of our common humanity. We can laugh at ourselves and with others, free of a judgmental spirit that is constantly sizing up one against the other. We are all in this together.

Although there is nothing like celebration for a bracing plunge into earthy and festive hilarity, there are all kinds of ways to retrain body and mind to lighten up. Volunteering to serve with those who teach preschoolers will refresh our spirits with the naturally unself-conscious play of little children, whose curiosity and enthusiasm are infectious. Pleasurable walks or bicycle rides can help us slow down and enjoy the simple goodness of bodily health and outdoor sights, sounds, and fragrances. Instead of praying with words, we can let the images of visual art or the wordless themes of instrumental music carry our heart to God.

Experimenting with the Disciplines helps us remember that it is not the form of practice but the substance of heart that matters. Trial and error reminds us that we are like children taking first steps. Sometimes we run ahead and stumble; other times we hesitate, waiting for the Divine Guide to beckon us forward. But we are always confident that the Holy Spirit is guiding us into all truth.

The saints were no strangers to innovation. Francis of Assisi reportedly told a brother who was exceedingly self-conscious to go make a fool of himself by preaching the Gospel naked. Now we might think that a bit drastic for the monk, if not for his listeners, but we can make the application without traveling quite so light.

I was sitting in the audience when a friend—a highly respected professor and theologian with a disarmingly humorous and down-to-earth manner—gave a lecture and then opened up the floor for questions and answers. The first person to the microphone proceeded to criticize everything he had just said, up one side and down the other. My friend paused and then, instead of defending himself, graciously thanked the "questioner." When I asked him about it later, he told me, "I'm practicing the Spiritual Discipline of not having to have the last word."

There is a dangerous liability in taking ourselves seriously, and it is no laughing matter to get free of it. Giving too much attention to our performance of the Disciplines puts us one step away from the slippery slope to self-righteousness. Jesus criticized the scribes and Pharisees for the heavy burdens they placed on others, exactly the opposite of the light yoke Jesus came to offer. These heavy burdens are the baggage of self-righteousness, the righteousness of the scribes and Pharisees. It is impossible to live lightly with God when we are dragging around our own religious pride.

One of the surest signs that we are taking our spiritual performance too seriously is when we start asking God to reward us for it. *I tried so hard today. Why didn't this turn out the way it was supposed to?* It is a subtle temptation to use Spiritual Disciplines as bargaining chips for getting what we want from God. *See how hard I prayed? Why didn't you answer me?* This is simply the way of legalism in another garb—if we follow the rules, then we have the right to expect that God will make reasonably sure life goes well.

These symptoms of self-righteousness easily escalate into a

full-blown case of spiritual entitlement. The Scripture is filled with stories of those who argued that their religious performance entitled them to better than what they were receiving at the hand of God.

Job's friend Eliphaz makes this very argument when he tries to offer an explanation for Job's catastrophic suffering. *You know that God does not punish innocent people,* Eliphaz says. *You have helped others get through hard times—but now that they are happening to you, why do you question God and wish you had never been born?* God destroys the wicked, not the righteous, Eliphaz contends. His argument is that when bad things happen to good people, it is because they have sinned and God is chastening them into repentance and correction. Eliphaz assures Job that he can count on God's deliverance because he is not a wicked person. Notice what Eliphaz offers as reassurance: "Is not your fear of God your confidence, and the integrity of your ways your hope?" (Job 4:6). As the basis for relief he appeals not to God's character, but to Job's piety. Eliphaz might as well have said, "God helps those who help themselves. You've helped yourself, Job, so you can expect God to help you."

We don't always recognize the subtle ways in which we demand that God "perform" in order to justify our obedience. But if we are willing to look, Scripture will hold up a mirror. For example, the history of Israel's relationship with God is our history, too. Consider what God says about the people through the prophet Isaiah: "Day after day they seek me and delight to know my ways, as if they were a nation that practiced righteousness and did not forsake the ordinance of their God; they ask of me righteous judgments, they delight to draw near to God" (Isa. 58:2). We would think that delighting to know God's ways and drawing near to God are just what God wants. Surely it must count for *something*.

The people cite these practices as evidence in defense of their demand for God to deliver them from suffering: "Why do we fast, but you do not see? Why humble ourselves, but you do not notice?" (Isa. 58:3). After all, they have been performing the very things God told them to do. Surely they should get points for obedience!

Yet listen to what God says next. Their obedience rings hollow because . . .

> Look, you serve your own interest on your fast day,
> and oppress all your workers. . . .
> Such fasting as you do today
> will not make your voice heard on high.
> Is such the fast that I choose,
> a day to humble oneself?
> Is it to bow down the head like a bulrush,
> and to lie in sackcloth and ashes?
> Will you call this a fast,
> a day acceptable to the Lord?
> Is not this the fast that I choose:
> to loose the bonds of injustice,
> to undo the thongs of the yoke,
> to let the oppressed go free,
> and to break every yoke? (Isa. 58:3–6)

The people did the right things at the right time, but for the wrong reasons. Their "obedience" was self-serving, not God-serving. Such a distorted perspective will corrupt any religious practice—a reminder yet again that practices in themselves have no worth. Authentic worship is a matter of the heart. It is not the discharge of religious duty. Self-righteousness will always weigh us down. Unable to abide in the True Vine, we are barren of the fruit of loving God in truth and justice.

The best antidote to taking ourselves too seriously is to take our focus off ourselves and place it on God. Indirection reminds us that we are not in control. We plant and water, but God grants the growth. It is God's life we are invited into, not a life we must create. This is rich, full, dynamic life, now and forever. It is not up to us—what words of freedom!

RELAXING AND REJOICING

When we focus on God instead of self, we find we can let go of the anxiety that had us in its grip: "Do not worry about anything, but in everything by prayer and supplication with thanksgiving let your requests be made known to God" (Phil. 4:6). As we simply and straightforwardly tell God our needs, we release the weight from our shoulders. It is God's now. God will guide us in what to do next, but the outcome rests in God's hands. Our spirit sighs in relief and gratitude. "For the LORD is good; his steadfast love endures forever, and his faithfulness to all generations" (Ps. 100:5).

The goodness of God is all around us, and if we take the smallest step toward it, it will come rushing in. This is where the

Disciplines are so helpful. They are not just abstract exercises for the "spiritual" part of our lives. They are embedded in the texture of everyday life. If we walk through our day in sensitivity to "Divine Breathings," we will receive guidance for practicing them—spontaneously, gratuitously. Planning is helpful, but we do not have to be on a program of practicing the Disciplines in order to weave them into our lives.

Here is a chance to give something away in secret—and we respond with inner rejoicing, knowing that we have just drained the power of greed and covetousness. Are we always pressed for time? Then here is a chance to waste time on purpose—to turn off the gadgets, quiet the voices of hurry, and reflect on the simple marvels of being alive: heart beating, lungs breathing, blood pulsing, a beautiful world in which to be a human being created to thrive in it.

For most of us, these are choices within our power to act on. Their very simplicity reminds us that the kingdom of God is near. The Lord is near. It is only the smallest step from the fretfulness of this world to the peace of God's presence. God is with us. Will we be with God?

Through indirection, we engage in the Disciplines not for themselves, but for what they open us to. Through the little acts of the Disciplines, we unlearn what comes automatically and relearn what does not. In time, we find that inwardly we are being transformed. Now we are more likely to see the person behind the counter as a human being rather than an object to get past so we can resume our agenda. It *is* our agenda to see her as a person who needs a friendly face instead of an impatient customer.

The Disciplines are constantly retraining us in awareness. Awareness gives rise to the little moments of sensing the grace of God in our lives. These moments become "little rejoicings" when we feel our spirit lift with the psalmist's to proclaim, "O give thanks to the LORD, for he is good; for his steadfast love endures forever" (Ps. 107:1). We are, blessedly, not in control. God is in control, and it is good. It is very good.

Here, then, is the fifth guideline for practicing the Disciplines in the way of freedom instead of the way of Law: relaxing and rejoicing. It is not up to us; it is up to God. One way or another, it will be okay. We will be okay. We are learning to relax in our relationship with God.

We read the Gospels free of expectation that we must be experts in understanding the text. Instead, we simply soak ourselves in the words and actions of Jesus with anticipation, knowing that the Spirit will implant the Word deep within heart and mind and soul.

We seek to acquire patience not by trying harder to be patient, which leads only to impatience. Instead, we seek opportunities to serve others, and we learn to pay careful attention to their needs, adjusting our ways to theirs, finding the rhythm of meeting them on their ground. And we learn patience as we take on the lowly way of the One who emptied himself in order to take on human form and serve us in love.

As we drain off the demands of self, the anxieties of our own needs, the second-guessing of our choices, we open up room deep within for reflection on the goodness of God. We have more opportunities to "taste and see that the LORD is good" (Ps 34:8). Our desire to be with God increases.

Even when the hard things of life bruise our spirit or tear away at our heart, we turn toward God—even if it is only to cry out *"why?"*—rather than reject God in bitterness. The effect of practicing the Disciplines has begun to take hold in deep change. All of life is being reoriented around the divine Center. When others turn away from God and the question Jesus asks his disciples is posed to us, "Do you also wish to go away?" we know we will answer with Peter: "Lord, to whom can we go? You have the words of eternal life" (John 6:67–68).

There are times when the circumstances of life impose a particular Discipline upon us, and this, too, becomes a chance to taste the goodness of God even through the harshness of life. Consider Jacob's son Joseph (see especially Gen. 35:22–26 and chapters 37, 39–45, and 50). Torn away from his family and imprisoned in Egypt, he accepted his circumstances as from the hand of God and lived accordingly. God honored his faithfulness, and he emerged a substantially formed, even transformed, person. A contemporary example is Nelson Mandela, who spent twenty-seven years in a South African prison for his opposition to apartheid. Afterward, he became the first democratically elected president of South Africa, a black man in what had formerly been the seat of the white man's power—presiding over a newly integrated society.

Another biblical example of an imposed discipline is Mary's pregnancy with Jesus. "Here am I, the servant of the Lord," she responds to her commission; "let it be with me according to your word" (Luke 1:38). To a significant degree her submission accounts for her great holiness. And Mary rejoices in the wondrous Magnificat: "My soul magnifies the Lord, and my spirit rejoices in God my Savior" (Luke 1:46–47).[27]

There is a remarkable depiction of an imposed Discipline of celebration in the beautiful film *Babette's Feast*,[28] based on a novella by Danish writer Isak Dinesen. The story takes place in a remote and windswept coastal community, among an austere and puritanical Protestant sect in the aftermath of its dour founder's passing. The founder's spinster daughters hire as a housekeeper Babette, a refugee from France, without knowing they have retained the services of a world-class chef. For years Babette keeps her artistry secret, cooking their bland diet of bread soup and boiled codfish. The ingrown community—hardened by fractious relationships, sorrow over betrayals and lost chances, and bitter regrets—maintains its colorless routines.

When Babette receives news that she has won the lottery in France, she offers to cook a feast in honor of the centennial anniversary of the founder's birth. The community reluctantly agrees, assuming it is a farewell gesture before she returns to her homeland. Their reluctance turns to fearful alarm when Babette spends sumptuously on luscious provisions. Boat after boat loads onshore such carnal delicacies as a live sea turtle, a calf's head, quail, cheeses and fruits, fine wine and champagne, and much more. One of the sisters has nightmares of a calf's head with the flames of hell licking up around it. The community privately vows among themselves to swallow the food and wine without tasting it. Pleasure is a sin!

When the evening comes for them to sit down at an exquisitely laid table and begin the feast, their pinched asceticism is undone by the lavishness of Babette's sacrificial gift. She has spent every last penny of her winnings on these culinary splendors. As they eat and drink of her labors of love, their hearts are softened and a great wave of healing sweeps over them. Bitter hurts dissolve in forgiveness. Fractured relationships are mended with tenderness. The proud are brought down and the lowly lifted up. The food and wine fill empty hearts as well as stomachs with good things.

Words are given to this sacramental experience by a military officer attending the dinner. He is back in town decades after falling in love with one of the founder's daughters. He left her in pursuit of glorious exploits and has agonized over his decision ever since. When he stands up to make a toast, he gives an eloquent speech about the eternal nature of grace that redeems lost chances and broken dreams. Babette's feast has drawn them into a celebration they had thought to refuse. But this celebration has opened up for them a life such as they have always longed for, but until now had never known. Their experience is testimony to the transforming power of these words from the Apostle Paul: "Whatever is true, whatever is honorable, whatever is just, whatever is pure, whatever is pleasing, whatever is commendable, if there is any excellence and if there is anything worthy of praise, think about these things" (Phil. 4:8).

The film's reversal of human experience from barrenness to fecundity is a parable of the kingdom of heaven. In the face of such marvels we exclaim with Paul, "Rejoice in the LORD always; again I will say, Rejoice" (Phil. 4:4). Jesus came proclaiming our immediate access to his Father's kingdom through him—the way, the truth, the life. This *life* is what we long for. It is the way into the all-inclusive community that genuinely unites and knits us together as one. It is the wholeness and holiness for which, by nature, our heart is hungering.

In the last chapter of this book, we will explore the power that ushers us into this life that is rooted in and blossoms from Love. This power is the very air we breathe in the kingdom of God, the living water we drink. It is the dynamic of the Spirit at work in our minds and hearts. It is what holds us when we let go of the flimsy raft of self-effort and entirely surrender ourselves to the mercy of God. It supernaturally charged the life of John Woolman so that he became a beacon of peace, justice, and compassion in his time and through the succeeding centuries. It will flow through us just as surely, sustaining us and empowering us: "You then, my child, be strong in the *grace* that is in Christ Jesus" (2 Tim. 2:1, emphasis added).

9

Living by Grace

From his fullness we have all received, grace upon grace.
—John 1:16

Christians need grace far more than "sinners." In the terrain of life with God, grace is not a ticket to heaven, but the earth under our feet on the road with Christ. It grounds us in reality and guides us along the path of discipleship. Grace saves us from life without God—even more, it empowers us for life with God.

We have no better example of "grace upon grace" in a human life than German martyr Dietrich Bonhoeffer, executed on April 9, 1945, just two weeks before Allied forces liberated the Flossenbürg concentration camp. Bonhoeffer conceived of relationship with God in terms of "'existence for others,' through participation in the being of Jesus"[29]—and then he blazed a trail of faithful and costly witness as he lived out that relationship in his life and in his death.

Grace sustained Bonhoeffer in his courageous decision to return to Germany from his study in the United States in order to share in the sufferings of his people. During his imprisonment from 1943 until 1945, he was able to call upon ingrained habits of virtue from years of daily spiritual practice. Consequently, his strength of character became a conduit for grace so empowering that he was able to conquer despair and offer himself in compassionate, sacrificial service to God's purposes for his life and death. On the day that he heard that the July 20, 1944 attempt to assassinate Hitler had failed—the day he knew that his own fate and the fate of his friends were sealed—he wrote an account of his life in the poem "Stations on the Road to Freedom."

> Wondrous transformation! Your strong and active hands
> are tied now. Powerless, alone, you see the end of your action.
> Still, you take a deep breath and lay your struggle for justice,
> quietly and in faith, into a mightier hand.
> Just for one blissful moment, you tasted the sweetness of free-
> dom,
> then you handed it over to God, that he might make it
> whole.[30]

Bonhoeffer's calm surrender in the shadow of death is overpowering testimony to the world of the reality of grace. On his way to the gallows he said to his friends, "This is the end—for me, a beginning," and then knelt in prayer before his hanging. A Nazi doctor in attendance that morning said, "I have hardly ever seen a man so submissive to the will of God."[31]

That moment when Bonhoeffer concluded one season of life and began another was a culmination of his long and steady obedience in the same direction. He had dedicated himself, body and soul, to the service of Christ. His personal habits of daily meditation, prayer, and sacrament were conscious actions taken for "a life of uncompromising adherence to the Sermon on the Mount in imitation of Christ."[32] His understanding of spiritual formation was assimilation "to the form of Christ in its entirety, the form of Christ incarnate, crucified and glorified. . . . 'Formation' . . . means in the first place Jesus' taking form in his church."[33]

Through Bonhoeffer's steady training in Spiritual Discipline, God so transformed his inward character that he was able to stand firm against the idolatrous cult of the Führer when so many around him were caught up in the seductive siren of patriotism. This is what enabled him to make the heart-wrenching decision to leave the security of the United States, where he had been doing postdoctoral work, so that he could stand in solidarity with his people against the gathering storm clouds of the Third Reich. This is what enabled him to describe (and truly experience) his imprisonment and suffering as a "wondrous transformation."

In Bonhoeffer's life and teachings we witness the difference between the soft complacency of "cheap grace" and the tough-minded discipleship of "costly grace." Cheap grace is "the preaching of forgiveness without requiring repentance, baptism without church discipline, Communion without confession, absolution without personal confession." True grace is "costly because it calls us to follow, and it is grace because it calls us to follow Jesus Christ. . . . It is costly because it compels a man to submit to the yoke of Christ and follow him; it is grace because Jesus says: 'My yoke is easy and my burden is light.'"[34]

Costly grace is the paradox of life with God freely offered to us, requiring only our decision to become participants instead of onlookers. "Saving" grace is how we begin inhaling the breath of

God—after that we continue breathing deeply and intentionally, taking in great lungfuls of sustaining grace like a 747 jumbo jet consuming fuel on takeoff.

THE FATHOMLESS WATERS OF LIFE

Bonhoeffer's life and death illustrate in the most vivid terms how the transformation of the human person leads to ever-deepening immersion in the fathomless waters of life with God. Few of us are asked to endure such an arduous and costly journey. Yet regardless of our circumstances, we face the same fundamental choice: to train for life in the kingdom of God, positioning ourselves to receive the gift of God's transforming work, cultivating attentiveness to Divine Breathings, immersing ourselves in the operations of Divine Love, seeking the kingdom of God over the kingdom of self, rejoicing in praise of "his glorious grace that he freely bestowed on us in the Beloved" (Eph. 1:6).

This is the marvelous goal and end result of all our engagement with the Scripture: to live off the grace of God free as birds of the air and splendid as lilies of the field, storing up treasures in heaven as the abiding place of our heart. God is in relentless pursuit of a People who will be gathered from the ends of the earth to join together in such a life, forming a community of love that is more powerful and glorious than all the kingdoms of this world.

We see this reality "through a glass darkly" now, but without the Bible we would not see it at all—or only in such fragments that we could never glimpse the whole. The whole becomes visible to us as we enter the world of the Bible expectantly, attentively, and humbly, recognizing the great Immanuel Principle—God with us—coursing through it. As we read with the heart, as we read with understanding, as we read together as a People, always we are encountering the Bible's question, which begs an answer: "I will be *with* you—will you be *with* Me?" As we choose to answer that question, we discover that God has been with us all along . . . and God will go ahead of us. In the prayer of Saint Patrick:

> *Christ be with me, Christ within me,*
> *Christ behind me, Christ before me,*
> *Christ beside me, Christ to win me,*
> *Christ to comfort and restore me.*
> *Christ beneath me, Christ above me,*
> *Christ in quiet, Christ in danger,*
> *Christ in hearts of all that love me,*
> *Christ in mouth of friend and stranger.*[35]

The only way we can "grow in the grace and knowledge of our Lord and Savior Jesus Christ" (2 Pet. 3:18) is to be in interactive relationship. This relationship is at the very center of the biblical story: divine initiative and human response. Divine mediation in human affairs takes place in order to allow human character to be developed. Human character is transformed in order to be *con*formed to divine Character. Grace entwines the two in an eternity of free interplay. Human personhood is never annihilated or dissolved, because the with God life is always and eternally a loving relationship, a community of loving persons with God as the very Center.

The foundational essence of grace can be expressed by *perichoresis,* a term used by the Greek fathers to describe the mutual interpenetration of the Trinity: Father, Son, and Holy Spirit in a joyous eternal communion expressed by individuality *and* mutuality. This is a relational intimacy of perfectly loving Persons. It is a divine Dance in the waters of Life, radiating outward like ripples on a pond until the entire surface is transformed by the movement at its Center.

Will we ever understand this relationship while we are still bound by the constraints of earthly existence? Not a chance! This wondrous mystery is a subject for eternal contemplation and celebration. But we can begin experiencing it now by saying *yes—I will be with You* in response to God's invitation. The mystery is not confusing. It is not a remote theological concept. It is, quite simply, the relational dynamic—or "perichoretic reality"—of living by grace.

The foundation of life with God is the dynamic interplay of Divine-human relationship, supremely revealed in the incarnation of Jesus Christ. Christ's life has become ours—signed, sealed, and delivered by grace. It is signed in the *definition* of grace: the reality of God's action in human lives. It is sealed by the manifest *reality* of grace: God's life is infused into human lives. And it is delivered by the *accessibility* of grace: it is open to all in Christ.

THE DEFINITION OF GRACE:
THE ACTION OF GOD IN OUR LIVES

The Bible reveals, first and last, that *grace is the action of God in our lives.* And this Divine action often occurs in the midst of ordinary life. When God appears to Abram and Sarah to announce that despite their advanced age they will bear a son—the promised offspring that had been only a far-off vision before now—the news is not broadcast supernaturally. No, in the way of God with human beings, it occurs in the middle of an otherwise ordinary day, embedded in familiar surroundings. Three visitors appear at the opening of Abram's tent by the oaks of Mamre, seeking a response within the cultural context of Near Eastern hospitality (see Gen. 18). They engage in the intimacy of meal sharing after Abram prepares a feast for them. Only then do they reveal the purpose of their Divine mission.

From this offspring will come the chosen People of God, and the house of David will be established. When David's heir, the promised Messiah, comes into the world, his appearance occurs in a lowly stable in the middle of an otherwise uneventful night, with a spectacular heavenly display visible only to simple shepherds in the hills.

God comes to us not to overwhelm us and overpower us, but to interrupt us in the midst of our ordinary routines, on the ground of what is familiar to us—everyday life, the arena in which most of life with God takes place. He whispers rather than shouts, gently prompts rather than shoves, *I am with you—will you be with Me?*

Always we are walking in the way of freedom, not coercion. The Bible does not in itself produce any magical effect. It reveals God's story that we might hear from the living God that this story is not only for a nomadic tribe thousands of years ago. It is not only for bands of persecuted followers of the Jesus way under threat from the Roman Empire. God's story is for all of us.

This is why Jesus took the Pharisees to task for studying the Scriptures without allowing God's life to penetrate their own:

"You have your heads in your Bibles constantly because you think you'll find eternal life there. But you miss the forest for the trees. These Scriptures are all about *me*! And here I am, standing right before you, and you aren't willing to receive from me the life you say you want" (John 5:39–40, *The Message*).

As Eugene Peterson comments, "To put it bluntly, not everyone who gets interested in the Bible and even gets excited about the Bible wants to get involved with God."[36] Reading the Bible to encounter the living God requires us to open our heart as well as our mind—to come to it with what Karl Barth calls "an honest, a fierce, seeking, asking, and knocking."[37]

Jesus assures us that our response to God's initiative will be answered by God's response. This is the assurance of grace: "Ask, and it will be given you; search, and you will find; knock, and the door will be opened for you. For everyone who asks receives, and everyone who searches finds, and for everyone who knocks, the door will be opened" (Matt. 7:7–8).

THE REALITY OF GRACE:
THE INFUSION OF GOD'S LIFE INTO OURS

Second, the Bible reveals grace as a Divine-human interplay in the manifest reality that *grace enables us to do with God what we could never do on our own.*

Frank Laubach, a pioneer of unceasing prayer and loving action, sank to the lowest pit of despondency on the brink of one of God's greatest transforming experiences in his life. Called to labor among the Filipino people on the island of Mindanao, he found himself one December evening on Signal Hill, where he walked each night after supper with his dog, Tip, to seek companionship with God. On this particular night in 1929, he was grieving over the province that seemed to be his defeat. Tears running down his cheeks, Tip nosing up under his arms to lick them off, he had a transforming experience best described in his own words:

> My lips began to move and it seemed to me that God was speaking.
>
> "My Child," my lips said, "you have failed because you do not really love these Moros. You feel superior to them because you are white. If you can forget you are an American and think only how I love them, they will respond."
>
> I answered back at the sunset, "God, I don't know whether you spoke to me through my lips, but if you did, it was the truth. . . . Drive me out of myself and come and take possession of me and think Thy thoughts in mine. . . ."
>
> My lips spoke to me again: "If you want the Moros to be fair to your religion, be fair to theirs. Study their Koran with them."[38]

Laubach obeyed and found his cottage crowded each night with local priests, Korans in hand, "bent upon making a Moslem out of me! So we went to work with great zeal."

This was the turning point. Laubach began to experience great infusions of grace—"After that night on Signal Hill, when God killed my racial prejudice and made me color-blind, it seemed as though He was working miracles at every turn." The reality of sustaining grace exploded into Laubach's soul, launching him into a vastly deeper and fuller spiritual life than he had ever known and spawning a literacy movement that eventually reached an estimated sixty million people.

Grace is the invisible made visible in ways we could never dream of, much less bring about. We know that grace is real because through divine empowerment, we find we are enabled to be and do in ways that would never be possible on our own.

Grace is a reality completely opposite to the realities of this world. The kingdom of this world operates on limited supply, competition for resources, an increasingly diminished and threatened environment. But grace operates like this: the more we use it, the more there is of it. No wonder Paul proclaims:

- we are justified "by his grace as a gift" (Rom. 3:24);

- we will receive "the abundance of grace" (Rom. 5:17);

- God is able "to provide you with every blessing in abundance, so that by always having enough of everything, you may share abundantly in every good work" (2 Cor. 9:8);

- we are able to be generous because of "the surpassing grace of God that he has given you" (2 Cor. 9:14);

- that we have redemption and forgiveness "according to the riches of his grace that he lavished on us" (Eph. 1:7–8);

- that God has made us alive together with Christ (by grace we have been saved) "so that in the ages to come he might show the immeasurable riches of his grace in kindness toward us in Christ Jesus" (Eph. 2:5–7).

THE ACCESSIBILITY OF GRACE:
IN CHRIST, OPEN TO ALL

God not only initiates and establishes relationship with us, God also guarantees that we are able to participate freely in this partnership. The third way in which living by grace reveals the relational dynamic at the heart of life with God is that *God makes grace accessible to us by empowering us with the means for growth*. As we have seen with the Disciplines, the means are not an imposed system of rules and routines, but freely offered ways of living a life. It is life God is after with us, not enforced obedience.

In our spiritual practice, we experience what the theologians call "prevenient grace"—meaning that our very desire to do what we can is prompted by God. God is at work in us to will and to act, drawing us, empowering us, transforming us. Therefore we learn by practicing the Spiritual Disciplines according to the law of liberty that they are first and last about God, because of God, through God. This is all grace. It is why Søren Kierkegaard, whose intellectual brilliance was matched only by the depths of his spiritual passion, became one of the most important voices in Christian history for drawing our attention first and last to what God has done for us.

Kierkegaard, whose misshapen body reinforced his profound sense of alienation from his fellow human beings, grew up in the desolate heath country of Jutland in western Denmark with an overbearing sense of dread. The condemnation of law lay heavy on his entire family because of his father's harsh and guilt-ridden piety, riveted on the doomsday vision that he would live to see all his children die in punishment for his sins of immorality. Yet

Kierkegaard would live to experience the astonishing reality of God's grace, so liberating him from the family curse and transforming his life that he could sum up spiritual transformation in these terms: "If I were to define Christian perfection, I should not say that it is a perfection of striving but specifically that it is the deep recognition of the imperfection of one's striving, and precisely because of this a deeper and deeper consciousness of the need for grace, not grace for this or that, but the infinite need infinitely for grace."[39]

Grace is not a system, but a way of life open to all people in the life of Jesus. The Apostle Peter proclaimed this good news in his precedent-setting visit to the house of Cornelius, a pious Gentile who was praying earnestly one day when a heavenly messenger visited him. "Cornelius, your prayer has been heard," the man in dazzling clothes assured him. Then he instructed Cornelius to summon Simon, who was called Peter, to his home, an unheard-of intimacy between Jew and Gentile. Peter's message proclaimed the grace of relationship for all people: "I truly understand that God shows no partiality, but in every nation anyone who fears him and does what is right is acceptable to him. You know the message he sent to the people of Israel, preaching peace by Jesus Christ—he is LORD of all" (see Acts 10:30–35). The experience of Cornelius was dramatic confirmation of Christ's own promise that when we seek, we will find.

THE GRACE OF TRANSFORMATION

In God's work of grace, the dynamic relationship of Divine-human interaction increasingly transforms us into the likeness of the One with whom we engage our lives. And, of course, while the Spiritual Disciplines are the foundational means for our formation, they are not the only means. Far from it. Sometimes God will use extraordinary circumstances, as in Bonhoeffer's life, or in extreme difficulties and trials we face, such as grave illness, the breakup of a family, the tragic loss of a loved one. More often God uses the ordinary circumstances of our everyday lives—the books we read, the conversations we have, the simple occurrences in the "little hours" of life.

The grace of transformation occurs in any and every arena. Sometimes God uses the interactive exchange that goes on between ourselves and the Holy Spirit in direct communion. Other times God uses physical means, such as the apparently random happenstance of circumstances, or human beings, whether friend, stranger, or enemy, to carry on this work. All of these things form and re-form us to the extent that we are willing participants in these arenas of grace. We can stop our growing conformity to Christ at any point, for God in sovereign wisdom has given us veto power over our own formation. Always, we are free moral agents with dignity established and continually affirmed by God.

The progressive transformation of our character increases our ability to receive grace upon grace. We know that the primary evidence of this character is summed up by "faith, hope, and love . . . and the greatest of these is love" (1 Cor. 13:13). Each of these qualities is the result of the dynamic interplay of God's life in our life.

Faith is the assurance of things hoped for; the conviction of things not seen (Heb. 11:1). Faith is choosing to make visible the invisible realities of the kingdom of God.

When the private letters of Mother Teresa were published posthumously,[40] the world learned about the inner life of a nun whose loving service to the poorest of the poor, the orphaned and the homeless, the sick and dying, made her an international icon of sacrificial compassion. The tireless work of this "living saint" over forty years in Calcutta, India, and abroad, through the order she founded, the Missionaries of Charity, garnered a multitude of awards, including the Nobel Peace Prize in 1979.

She keenly felt the "not seen" and the lack of "assurance"—but she lived out her faith in her actions, not in her feelings. Although she was afflicted with feeling invisible to God, she was making God visible to others in her faithful practice of service. This is what self-identified atheist Christopher Hitchens[41] missed when he reviewed her private writings and proclaimed her "a confused old lady [who] for all practical purposes had ceased to believe."[42] Without faith, there would have been no life. Mother Teresa had much more of the presence of Christ in her life than she realized. To the forgotten, the despised, the neglected, she *was* Christ. To a world that is trained to ignore and judge and hate, she is an astonishment—unbelievably so, for an atheist.

Faith is the willingness to trust that God is at work. In the worst of suffering and misery, where Mother Teresa spent most of her life, faith is the willingness to suspend disbelief that the world has been abandoned by God. In faith, we accept the news that God has come to us. We choose to enter into the story of God with us, believing that we are a People chosen by God to reveal the love of God for the whole world.

Faith gives rise to hope, which is the refusal to accept the world at face value. Bonhoeffer paid with his life for his refusal. Mother

Teresa paid for her refusal outwardly with a life given away in service and inwardly with a life torn by anguished hope. But "in hope we were saved," explains Paul. "Now hope that is seen is not hope. For who hopes for what is seen? But if we hope for what we do not see, we wait for it with patience" (Rom. 8:24–25).

As we respond in trust that God will accomplish the transformation of our character, our hearts will be "strengthened by grace" (Heb. 13:9), so that we might live more fully with God. Paul's great progression in Romans chapter 5 declares the synergistic power of our "peace with God" through the justification of faith in Christ, which gives us access to "this grace in which we stand" and enables us to "boast in our hope of sharing the glory of God" (verses 1–2). "And not only that, but we also boast in our sufferings, knowing that suffering produces endurance, and endurance produces character, and character produces hope, and hope does not disappoint us, because God's love has been poured into our hearts through the Holy Spirit that has been given to us" (verses 3–5).

Love is the character of God, the eternal reality into which we are transformed, the great gift that our transformation enables us to give and receive in increasingly deeper measure. No human accomplishment, no spiritual practice, no divine utterance, no life of toil for God—nothing we can possibly do matters unless we do it with God, and therefore with love (see 1 Cor. 13:1–3).

Mother Teresa described her life work with the Missionaries of Charity as "God's Love in action with the poorest of the poor." She lived out the teaching of the Apostle John in his first epistle, which reverberates with the theme of love in echoes of the fourth Gospel: "For this is the message you have heard from

the beginning, that we should love one another" (1 John 3:11).
Mother Teresa knew with every fiber in her body that John's call
to love does not refer to some warm feeling or abstract ideal. She
demonstrated, at great cost to her own comfort and feelings, that
love involves clearheaded action toward God and others, rooted
in Jesus' sacrificial action on our behalf.

The relational reality of grace is revealed in John's emphasis
that our love is not an originating love, but a responding love:
"We love because he first loved us" (1 John 4:19). And the active
nature of grace is revealed in John's teaching about what love
looks like in action: "We know love by this, that he laid down his
life for us—and we ought to lay down our lives for one another.
How does God's love abide in anyone who has the world's goods
and sees a brother or sister in need and yet refuses help?" (1 John
3:16–17). No teaching could be more straightforward or clear
than that. Or this: "Little children, let us love, not in word or
speech, but in truth and action" (1 John 3:18).

Grace is the activity of God in our lives, the reality of God
pouring into us more than we could ever do on our own, the love
of God pursuing us, supporting us, changing us, upholding us,
uniting us, sending us. "Changed from glory into glory, 'til in
heaven we take our place, 'til we cast our crowns before Thee,
lost in wonder, love, and praise."[43]

Because of God's great love, grace creates a thin space in which
the visible realities of this world are charged with the invisible
reality of Love. Doubt is overcome by faith; despair is overcome by
hope; brutality and loneliness are conquered by love. The poor in
spirit receive the kingdom of heaven. Those who mourn are com-
forted. The meek inherit the earth. Those who hunger and thirst

for righteousness are filled. The merciful receive mercy. The pure in heart see God. The peacemakers are called the children of God. Those who are persecuted for righteousness' sake receive the kingdom of heaven, a realm of gladness and rejoicing.

GRACE IS FOR LIFE

Living by grace is essential for life. We are "labourers together with God," as Paul says (1 Cor. 3:9, kjv). While we are reading the Bible with God, it is always God acting. When we are living based on the truth proclaimed in the Bible, we are living off of the resources of God's action in our lives. We do what we can, and God accomplishes what we cannot, but it is all grace because we are doing everything in cooperation. It is grace because it spills over into every part of our lives. When we are at home, we are acting with God. When we are with children, we are acting with God. When we are at work, we are acting with God. When we are at rest, we are acting with God.

Do we feel sometimes that we are living on too little grace? Grace is here, waiting for us to take our next deep breath with the simple prayer, "Lord, help me to act with you in this." Grace is here to empower us, pouring forth as we open ourselves with the simple request, "Lord, help me to rely upon your strength to do this." We are saved by grace in order to live by grace. This carries over into the next life—grace just increases, so better that we get used to it now!

Grace entwines the Divine-human interplay of spiritual formation. So it is not accessible to us if we are trying to act independently. Oh, there is plenty we can do in the flesh, if we want to.

But why work hard to build on "wood, hay, [and] straw" instead of the foundation of "gold, silver, [and] precious stones" (1 Cor. 3:12)? When we act with God, under grace, the results are imperishable treasure that will last into eternity. Our lives need not feel useless and futile. The treasure of grace is only a breath away.

This does not mean we are free from struggle and doubt. As with Mother Teresa's dark night of the soul, it takes effort— sometimes, agonizing effort—to accept the ways of God mediated through the ways of humankind. But the struggle itself is transforming, for it compels us to *act* on our desire for God.

Even when grace rains down on us, we cannot take it in if we turn our collar against it and bury our face inside protective garments. We must instead turn our face upward, open our mouth, and drink it in. God's grace is waiting for us in the Bible— indeed, everywhere—but it will come neither instantly nor easily. However, it will always come when we want it enough to seek it with all our heart.

Paul gives us word pictures to help us understand the transforming nature of grace. To the Galatians, he exclaims that he is in "the pain of childbirth until Christ is formed in you" (Gal. 4:19). To the Romans he affirms "those whom [God] foreknew he also predestined to be conformed to the image of his Son" (Rom. 8:29). To the Corinthians he proclaims, "All of us, with unveiled faces, seeing the glory of the LORD as though reflected in a mirror, are being transformed into the same image from one degree of glory to another; for this comes from the LORD, the Spirit" (2 Cor. 3:18).

All this *forming, conforming,* and *transforming* in our hearts and minds and souls comes from this life that is beyond ourselves but now available to us through the life, death, and resurrection of Jesus Christ: "There is therefore now no condemnation for those who are in Christ Jesus. For the law of the Spirit of life in Christ Jesus has set you free from the law of sin and of death" (Rom. 8:1–2). Paul uses a specific word here to identify the secret of our life that is hidden with God in Christ: *zoë*, the eternal, uncreated life that originates in God alone.

Let's be very clear about the role of the Bible here. The Bible is not the life. *Zoë* resides in God alone. But the Bible is a reliable guide into this *zoë* life.

Scripture identifies two kinds of life: *bios*, the physical, created life; and *zoë*, the spiritual, eternal life. Likewise, Scripture identifies two kinds of death: *teleute,* physical death; and *thanatos,* spiritual death. So it is entirely possible to be physically alive but spiritually dead. God's *zoë* floods our lives with Christ's life, forming us into radical communities of his disciples who are empowered to express his life and love through our own lives, individually and corporately.

This is the life to which Jesus refers when he announces that he came so we might have "life, and have it abundantly" (John 10:10). It is the life announced by John, as he testifies, "God gave us eternal life, and this life is in his Son" (1 John 5:11). It is the life that saves us: "For if while we were enemies, we were reconciled to God through the death of his Son," says Paul, "much more surely, having been reconciled, will we be saved by his life" (Rom. 5:10). It is the life that in all its fullness awaited Bonhoeffer as he crossed over from this one, leading him to whisper to his friends his final words, "This is the end, for me a beginning."

Life, life, life. It pulsates throughout the Bible, flowing from the living Word. The apostles declared that we are being saved by Christ's life, and his resurrection convinced them that this *zoë* life was indestructible. The glorious words *He is risen!* proved to them that the new life, which had been ever-present with them in the person and teachings of Jesus, could not be destroyed by killing the body.

This *life* continues on: no human or demonic power can overcome it. The gates of hell will not prevail against it. This unquenchable, indestructible *zoë* is offered by Jesus to all who trust in him. The greatest eschatological fact of all time is the resurrection, for it ushered in a new order of life, available to everyone: "Christ in you, the hope of glory" (Col. 1:27). Christ in us; us in Christ; a new order of life from above. Paul states it ever so succinctly in Colossians 3:4: "Christ, who is your *zoë.*"

This salvation in Jesus Christ is only for participants. It is not for mere observers, nor is it for consumers. "Consumer Christianity" is a contradiction in terms. The consumer approach attempts to seize it as "*my* life—I will utilize this with-God life to suit my needs and my purposes." Now, I hate to be blunt about it, but this *zoë* life simply doesn't work that way. If I am to enter into the eternal, uncreated life that originates in God alone, I must surrender my life. When I enter the with-God life, it is not my life anymore; it is Christ's life, in which I am privileged to become a participant.

And what a life it is! It is as virulent as AIDS. But instead of infecting us with death, it consumes us with the life for which we were made. That is because *zoë* has a principle of its own; no human being can control it. It forms us into Christlikeness—irresistibly, overwhelmingly, inevitably, relentlessly.

When we are helping a baby learn to walk, we don't give her an instruction book. We offer protection and encouragement as she does what comes naturally. When the time is right, the principle of life in that little one will compel her to walk. When she finally takes off on her own, in triumph and joy, it is a glorious sight.

In much the same way, this *zoë* that we receive from God *will* accomplish its work—we can count on it. God invites us—indeed, commands us—to seek this life out, to pursue it, to turn into it, because there is also within us the principle of death, stemming from the Fall. It is not nearly as powerful as *zoë*, but it wars against the principle of life with an all-out attack, prowling around like a roaring lion, looking for someone to devour (see 1 Pet. 5:6). It is ferocious, and therefore we must constantly be saying *yes* to life and *no* to death. We must always be discerning life-giving actions and attitudes from those that are death-giving. We must forever be "turning, turning, turning, 'til we come round right," as the old Shaker hymn puts it.

A GREAT CROWD ASSEMBLED

One day there will be a great crowd assembled on "the mountain of the Lord" (Mic. 4:2). Gathered there to learn God's ways and walk in God's paths will be People from every tongue and nation of the earth, from every tribe and tradition. Each of us will be a distinct note of grace as together we form the melodies and chords swirling throughout the assembled throng. Only together will we hear the mighty song that the Spirit of God is singing through the People of God.

This is a bit of what the glorious reality of God's loving community will be like. We can taste it now by entering the Bible in order to plunge our dry lives into the great river of life with God. And just as surely as rivers run toward the sea, this vision will sweep us into the practice of life with God, for we will no longer be satisfied to stand on the banks and watch others swim past.

We know that one day, God will bring us into fullness of life in the divine Center. The book of Revelation envisions the completion of God's plan for humanity and the extension of human existence on into eternity. It shows us the cosmic character of Christ, who promises to be with us "always, to the end of the age" (Matt. 28:20), and of the Lord God Almighty, who has always been present in human history, suffering with us, rejoicing with us, wooing us, sustaining us.

The efforts of God are culminating in the gathering of an obedient, disciplined, freely gathered People who know in our day (and will know fully in the days to come) the life and powers of the kingdom of God. This community is a People of cross and crown, of courageous action and sacrificial love, who will come to fulfillment beyond time in the formation of a new heaven and new earth teeming with perfectly loving people. Old ways of dominance, alienation, travail, suffering, and mortality will give way to life eternal. Worship of self will disappear along with temporal things, giving way utterly to joyous, unending worship of God. "The leaves of the tree [will be] for the healing of the nations. Nothing accursed will be found there any more. But the throne of God and of the Lamb will be in it, and his servants will worship him; they will see his face" (Rev. 22:2–4).

Even now we are part of this calling forth of the all-inclusive community of loving persons that God has been intent upon forming throughout all of history. To all who long to be part of this eternal community,

> The Spirit and the bride say, "Come."
> And let everyone who hears say, "Come."
> And let everyone who is thirsty come.
> Let anyone who wishes take the water of life as a gift.
> (Rev. 22:17)

THE DYNAMIC OF SPIRITUAL TRANSFORMATION

Stage of Formation	Scriptures	God's Action	Human Reaction
I. The People of God in Individual Communion	Genesis 1–11*	Creates, instructs, steward of a good creation, banishes, destroys, restores	Disobey, rebel, sacrifice, murder, repent, obey
II. The People of God Become a Family	Genesis 12–50	Gives promise and establishes Abrahamic covenant, makes a great people	Faith, wrestle with God, persevere
III. The People of God in Exodus	Exodus, Leviticus, Numbers, Deuteronomy	Extends mercy, grace, and deliverance from exile; delivers the Mosaic covenant/law	Obey and disobey, develop a distinctive form of ritual
IV. The People of God in the Promised Land	Joshua, Judges, Ruth, 1 Samuel 1–12	Establishes a theocracy, bequeaths the Promised Land	Inhabit the Promised Land, accept judges as mediators
V. The People of God as a Nation	1 Samuel 13–31 & 2 Samuel, 1 & 2 Kings, 1 & 2 Chronicles, 1 Esdras 1	Permits the monarchy, exalts good kings, uses secular nations for blessing	Embrace the monarchy
VI. The People of God in Travail	Job, Psalms of Lament, Ecclesiastes, Lamentations, Tobit	Permits tribulation, allows suffering to strengthen faith	Complain yet remain faithful
VII. The People of God in Prayer and Worship	Psalms, Psalm 151	Establishes liturgical worship	Praise, prayer
VIII. The People of God in Daily Life	Proverbs, Ecclesiastes, Song of Solomon, Wisdom of Solomon, The Wisdom of Jesus Son of Sirach (Ecclesiasticus)	Gives precepts for living in community	Teachable, learning, treasure beautiful words and artistic expression

IN THE WITH-GOD LIFE: FIFTEEN EXPRESSIONS

Type of Mediation	Locus of Mediation	Social Context	Central Individual(s)	Key Spiritual Disciplines
Face-to-face	Garden, field, Noah's ark	Individuals	Adam, Eve, Enoch, Noah	Practicing the Presence, confession, sacrifice, obedience/submission
Through the family	Tent, desert, jail	Extended families and nomadic clans	Abraham and Sarah, Isaac, Jacob, Joseph	Pilgrimage, sacrifice, chastity
Through God's terrifying acts and the Law	Ark of the covenant, tabernacle	Nomadic tribes	Moses	Submission, silence, simplicity, worship
Through the conquest and learning to act with God	Shiloh, Bethel	An ethnic people with fluid leadership	Joshua, Deborah, Ruth, Samson, Gideon, Samuel	Guidance, radical obedience/submission, secrecy
Through the king, prophets, priests, and sacrifices	Altars, consecrated places, first (Solomonic) temple	Political nation on the world stage	Saul, David, Hezekiah, Elijah, Elisha	Worship, prayer
Through suffering and the disappointments of life	Ash heap, hard circumstances of life	Individual	Job, Israel as the suffering servant	Fasting, solitude, silence, submission, service, celebration
Through song, prayer, worship	Jerusalem, flowering of individual experience	Nation	David	Prayer, worship, confession, celebration, meditation
Through wisdom	Temple, in the gate, home	Nation triumphant	Solomon	Study, guidance, celebration, meditation

Stage of Formation	Scriptures	God's Action	Human Reaction
IX. The People of God in Rebellion	1 Kings 12–2 Kings 25:10, 2 Chronicles 10–36:19, Isaiah, Jeremiah 1–36, Hosea, Joel, Amos, Jonah, Micah, Nahum, Habakkuk, Zephaniah, Judith, Prayer of Manasseh	Proclaims prophetic judgment and redemption, reveals his rule over all nations, promises Immanuel, uses secular nations to bring judgment	Disbelieve and reject, believe false prophets, a faithful remnant emerges
X. The People of God in Exile	2 Kings 25:11–30, 2 Chronicles 36:20–23, Jeremiah 37–52, Lamentations, Ezekiel, Daniel, Obadiah, Baruch, Letter of Jeremiah, Additions to Daniel	Judges, yet remains faithful to covenant promises	Mourn, survive, long for Jerusalem, stand for God without institutions
XI. The People of God in Restoration	Ezra, Nehemiah, Esther, Daniel, Haggai, Zechariah, Malachi, Additions to Esther, 1 Esdras 2–9, & 2 Esdras, 1, 2, 3, & 4 Maccabees, Tobit, Additions to Daniel	Regathers and redeems, restructures social life	Return, obey, rebuild, worship, pursue Messianic figure, compile Septuagint
XII. The People of God with Immanuel	Matthew, Mark, Luke, John	Sends the Son and acts with the Son	Hear and follow, resist and reject
XIII. The People of God in Mission	Acts	Sends the Holy Spirit and creates the Church	Believe and proclaim, disbelieve and persecute
XIV. The People of God in Community	Romans, 1 & 2 Corinthians, Galatians, Ephesians, Philippians, Colossians, 1 & 2 Thessalonians, 1 & 2 Timothy, Titus, Philemon, Hebrews, James, 1 & 2 Peter, 1, 2, & 3 John, Jude	Builds, nurtures, and mobilizes the Church	Become disciples of Jesus Christ and make disciples to the ends of the earth
XV. The People of God into Eternity	Revelation	Reveals infinite progress toward infinite good	Worship and praise, creativity that magnifies God

Type of Mediation	Locus of Mediation	Social Context	Central Individual(s)	Key Spiritual Disciplines
Through the prophets and repression by the Gentiles	High places, Temple desecrated and destroyed	Nation under siege and dispersed	Isaiah, Hosea, Amos	Fasting, repentance, obedience/ submission, solitude, silence, the law internalized
Through punishment, being a blessing to their captors	Babylon, anyplace, anytime	Ethnics abroad without a political homeland	Ezekiel, Jeremiah	Detachment, fasting, simplicity, prayer, silence, service
Through repentance, service, synagogue study	Rebuilt Temple, synagogue	Remnant on the international scene, ethnics in the leadership of other nations	Ezra, Cyrus the Persian, Nehemiah, Maccabees, Essenes, John the Baptist	Pilgrimage, confession, worship, study, service
Through the Incarnate Word and the living presence of the kingdom	Temple and synagogue, boats and hillsides, gatherings of disciples	Small groups, disciples, apostles, hostile critics	Jesus Christ Incarnate	Celebration, study, pilgrimage, submission, prayer, sacrifice, obedience, confession
Through the Holy Spirit, persecution, and martyrdom	Temple, synagogue, schools, riversides, public square	Jew, Gentile, house churches, abandonment of social strata	Peter, Paul	Speaking and hearing the word, sacrifice, guidance, generosity/ service, fasting, prayer
In one another, through Scripture, teaching, preaching, prophetic utterance, pastoral care, the Holy Spirit, the sacraments	Gathered community	Community redefined by the Body of Christ, decadent Greco-Roman culture	Peter, Paul, John	Prayer, study, accountability/ submission, fellowship
Throughout the cosmos	Focused in the New Jerusalem and extending throughout the cosmos	The Trinity and its community	God the Father, Son, and Holy Spirit; apostles, prophets	Living beyond disciplines

AN OVERVIEW OF GOD'S PURPOSE OF
TRANSFORMATION IN HISTORY

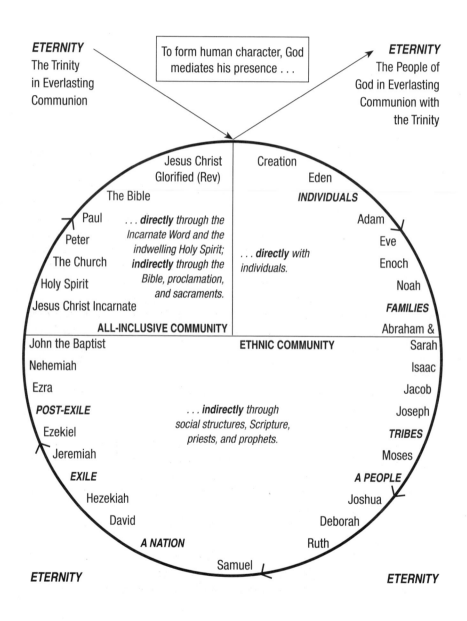

ETERNITY
The Trinity
in Everlasting
Communion

To form human character, God
mediates his presence . . .

ETERNITY
The People of
God in Everlasting
Communion with
the Trinity

Jesus Christ
Glorified (Rev)

Creation
Eden

The Bible

INDIVIDUALS

Paul

. . . *directly* through the
Incarnate Word and the
indwelling Holy Spirit;
indirectly through the
Bible, proclamation,
and sacraments.

Adam

Peter

Eve

The Church

. . . *directly* with
individuals.

Enoch

Holy Spirit

Noah

Jesus Christ Incarnate

FAMILIES

ALL-INCLUSIVE COMMUNITY

Abraham &

John the Baptist

ETHNIC COMMUNITY

Sarah

Nehemiah

Isaac

Ezra

Jacob

POST-EXILE

. . . *indirectly* through
social structures, Scripture,
priests, and prophets.

Joseph

Ezekiel

TRIBES

Jeremiah

Moses

EXILE

A PEOPLE

Hezekiah

Joshua

David

Deborah

A NATION

Ruth

Samuel

ETERNITY

ETERNITY

Notes

1. Adapted from the *Renovaré Spiritual Formation Bible,* a chart displaying the full sweep of biblical history across fifteen expressions of how God is *with* God's people is reprinted as a chart on pages 202–205 of this book.
2. There are many helpful plans offering multiple options for regular Bible reading. Such resources are available from charitable organizations, churches and Christian schools, multiple resources on the Internet, or packaged in Bibles available for purchase on bookstore shelves. For help in understanding difficult passages or learning about the historical and linguistic contexts for books and passages, it is also helpful to have a comprehensive study Bible or a good Bible handbook or general commentary for easy reference.
3. Dallas Willard, *Hearing God: Developing a Conversational Relationship with God,* originally published as *In Search of Guidance* (Downers Grove, IL: Inter-Varsity Press, 1999), p. 142.
4. Karl Barth, *The Word of God and the Word of Man* (Gloucester, MA: Peter Smith, 1978), p. 28.
5. From the hymn "Turn Your Eyes upon Jesus," lyrics by Helen H. Lemmel.
6. Lyrics by Alexander Groves in public domain, "Break Thou the Bread of Life."
7. A *lectionary* is a schedule of appointed readings tied to seasons of the church year and adapted to the specific celebrations and observances of a particular church tradition. In the liturgical stream of Christianity, the lectionary is intended to guide the people of God throughout the entire Bible together, in one- to three-year cycles.
8. *The Confessions of St. Augustine,* trans. Rex Warner (New York: New American Library/Mentor, 1963), VIII.12, pp. 181–83.
9. Albert Outler, a United Methodist theologian and Wesley scholar, developed the idea of the quadrilateral in the 1960s as a way of summarizing Wesley's theology. Donald A. D. Thorson explains: "The 'Wesleyan quadrilateral' is a

paradigm, or model, of how Wesley conceived of the task of theology" (*The Wesleyan Quadrilateral,* Grand Rapids, MI: Zondervan, 1990, p. 21).

10. From the hymn "Break Thou the Bread of Life," lyrics by Mary A. Lathbury.

11. This visual demonstration of the concept of "emergence" can be found in D. Marr, *Vision* (New York: W. H. Freeman, 1982), p. 101, Figure 3–1, where it is attributed to R. C. James.

12. Metropolitan Anthony of Sourozh, in "I Believe in God," by William Barclay, Colin Brown, and Anthony Bloom, ed. Rupert E. Davies (London: Westminster Press, 1968), posted online at www.metropolit-anthony.orc.ru/eng/eng_04.htm.

13. Dallas Willard, *Renovation of the Heart* (Colorado Springs: NavPress, 2002), p. 103. Scripture citations are from the NRSV.

14. For the origins of this phrase, see: E. Y. Mullins, *The Axioms of Religion* (Philadelphia: The Griffith & Rowland Press, 1908), p. 67; and *The Theological Works of the Rev. John Howard Hinton, M.A.*, Vol. I—Systematic Divinity (London: Houlston & Wright, 1864), I:455–59.

15. From Francis Thompson, "The Hound of Heaven," in *The Oxford Book of English Mystical Verse* (London: Oxford, 1917), #239.

16. Peter Gomes, *The Good Book: Reading the Bible with Mind and Heart* (New York: Avon, 1996), p. 14.

17. Eugene Peterson, *Eat this Book* (Grand Rapids, MI: Eerdmans, 2006), p. 104.

18. Archbishop of Canterbury Rowan Williams, "Larkin Student Lecture: The Bible Today, Reading and Hearing," presented at the University of Toronto, Canada, 16 April 2007.

19. Richard Foster, *Streams of Living Water* (San Francisco: HarperOne, 1998). If you are familiar with this book, you will recognize these as the "Streams" I deal with there at far greater length.

20. Phoebe Palmer, *Selected Writings,* ed. Thomas C. Oden (New York: Paulist, 1988), p. 115.

21. Material on the *charismata* is adapted directly from Richard Foster's *Streams of Living Water,* pp. 125–26.

22. See Leviticus chapter 25 for understanding the Hebrew Year of Jubilee, a "Sabbath year" God commanded the people to observe that would transform and renew their life together.

23. Foster, *Streams of Living Water,* p. 12.

24. Foster, *Streams of Living Water,* pp. 14–15.

25. Dallas Willard, *The Spirit of the Disciplines* (San Francisco: HarperOne, 1992), p. 153.

26. Willard, *Spirit of the Disciplines,* pp. 137–38. Italics in the original.

27. It is important to sound an urgent word of caution here. God never intends that we suffer physical, psychological, or spiritual harm as Discipline. These factors may be present as unavoidable risks under certain circumstances im-

posed by others, such as Joseph's enslavement by his brothers. His brothers meant him harm, but God did not. A woman in an abusive relationship should not consider it an imposed Discipline to which she ought to submit— she should get out of the relationship and run for her life! What is imposed on us is not the evils of this world, but the necessity of choosing how we will respond to them.

28. Screenplay and direction by Gabriel Axel, 1987, Danish and French with English subtitles.

29. Dietrich Bonhoeffer, *Letters and Papers from Prison,* enlarged ed., ed. Eberhard Bethge, trans. R. H. Fuller, John Bowden, et al. (New York: Macmillan, 1971), pp. 380–83.

30. Translated from *Widerstand und Ergebung,* pp. 403–4, as cited in *A Testament to Freedom: The Essential Writings of Dietrich Bonhoeffer,* ed. Geffrey B. Kelly and F. Burton Nelson (San Francisco: HarperOne, 1990), pp. 542–43.

31. The definitive account of Bonhoeffer's life is Eberhard Bethge's *Dietrich Bonhoeffer: A Biography,* ed. Victoria J. Barnett (Minneapolis: Augsburg Fortress, 2000). The citation here may also be found in an overview of Bonhoeffer's life drawn from a variety of sources and posted at the online site of the U.S. Holocaust Memorial Museum, http://www.ushmm.org/museum/exhibit/online/bonhoeffer/b6.htm#21r.

32. Dietrich Bonhoeffer, *Gesammelte Schriften, III,* 2nd ed. (Munich: Kaiser Verlag, 1965–69), pp. 25, as cited in Bethge, *Dietrich Bonhoeffer: A Biography,* p. 380.

33. Dietrich Bonhoeffer, *The Cost of Discipleship,* trans. R.H. Fuller, rev. ed. (New York: Macmillan, 1963), p. 341.

34. Bonhoeffer, *The Cost of Discipleship,* pp. 45, 47.

35. From hymn lyrics by Cecil Francis Alexander, 1889, translated from the original Gaelic poem "Saint Patrick's Lorica."

36. Peterson, *Eat this Book,* p. 30.

37. Barth, *The Word of God and the Word of Man,* p. 87.

38. Frank C. Laubach, *Thirty Years with the Silent Billion: Adventuring in Literacy* (Old Tappan, NJ: Revell, 1960), pp. 26–28.

39. Søren Kierkegaard, "Grace More Rigorous than Law," in Howard Hong and Edna Hong, eds., *Søren Kierkegaard's Journals and Papers* (Bloomington, IL: Indiana University Press, 1970), p. 170.

40. Mother Teresa and Brian Kolodiejchuk, *Mother Teresa: Come Be My Light* (New York: Doubleday, 2007).

41. Journalist and author of multiple books including his bestselling *God Is Not Great: How Religion Poisons Everything* (New York: Hachette Book Group, 2007).

42. Christopher Hitchens, "The Dogmatic Doubter," *Newsweek* (10 September 2007), p. 41.

43. From the hymn "Love Divine, All Love Excelling," lyrics by Charles Wesley.

For Further Reading

Bible References

Achtemeier, Paul J. *HarperCollins Bible Dictionary,* rev. San Francisco: HarperOne, 1996.

Beitzel, Barry J. *Biblica: A Social and Historical Journey through the Lands of the Bible.* Hauppauge, NY: Barron's Educational Series, 2007.

Bromiley, Geoffrey W. *The International Standard Bible Encyclopedia,* 4 vols. Grand Rapids, MI: Eerdmans, 1995.

Brown, Raymond E., et al. *The New Jerome Bible Handbook.* Collegeville, MN: Liturgical Press, 1992.

Brueggeman, Walter. *Theology of the Old Testament: Testimony, Dispute, Advocacy.* Minneapolis: Fortress, 1997.

Heschel, Abraham. *The Prophets.* Peabody, MA: Hendrickson Publishers, 2007.

Pritchard, James. *The Harper Collins Concise Atlas of the Bible.* San Francisco: HarperOne, 1997.

Commentaries

Barclay, William. *Barclay's Guide to the New Testament.* Louisville, KY: Westminster, 2008.

Calvin, John. *Calvin's Commentaries,* 22 vols. Grand Rapids: Baker, 2005.

Brown, Raymond Edward, Joseph A. Fitzmyer, and Roland Edmund Murphy, eds., *The New Jerome Biblical Commentary.* Englewood Cliff, NJ: Prentice Hall, 1989.

The Word Biblical Commentary Series, 58 vols. Nashville: Thomas Nelson. (Authors and publication dates vary by volume.)

Principles of Biblical Interpretation

Berkhof, L. *Principles of Biblical Interpretation.* Grand Rapids: Baker Book House, 1967.

Bright, John. *The Authority of the Old Testament.* London, UK: S.C.M. Press, 1967.

Fuller, Daniel P. *The Unity of the Bible: Unfolding God's Plan for Humanity.* Grand Rapids: Zondervan, 2000.

Rowley, Harold Henry. *The Unity of the Bible.* Westport, CT: Greenwood Press Reprint, 1978.

Books on Spiritual Formation and the Spiritual Disciplines

Foster, Richard J. *Celebration of Discipline: The Path to Spiritual Growth.* San Francisco: HarperOne, 1978.

_____. *Streams of Living Water.* San Francisco: HarperOne, 1998.

Willard, Dallas. *The Divine Conspiracy.* San Francisco: HarperOne, 1998.

_____. *The Spirit of the Disciplines: Understanding How God Changes Lives.* San Francisco: HarperOne, 1988.

Books on the Dynamics of Life with God

Augustine. *The Confessions of St. Augustine.* Orleans, MA: Paraclete, 1986.

Bonhoeffer, Dietrich. *The Cost of Discipleship.* New York: MacMillan, 1963.

_____. *Life Together.* New York: Simon & Schuster, Touchstone, 1995.

Brother Lawrence, *Practicing the Presence of God.* Trans. John J. Delaney. New York: Doubleday, 1977.

Caussade, Jean-Pierre de. *The Sacrament of the Present Moment.* San Francisco: HarperOne, 1982.

Guyon, Madame Jeanne. *Experiencing the Depths of Christ.* Jacksonville, FL: Christian Books, Seedsowers, 1981.

Heschel, Abraham. *God in Search of Man: A Philosophy of Judaism.* New York: Farrar, Straus, and Giroux, 1976.

_____. *Man Is Not Alone: A Philosophy of Religion.* New York: Farrar, Straus, and Giroux, 1976.

Kelley, Thomas. *A Testament of Devotion.* San Francisco: HarperOne, 1996.

Laubach, Frank C. *Letters by a Modern Mystic.* Colorado Springs, CO: Purposeful Design Publications, 2007.

Rilke, Rainer Maria. *The Book of Hours.* Barrows and Macy, contributors. New York: Riverhead, 2005.

Thomas à Kempis. *The Imitation of Christ.* Trans. William C. Creasy. Notre Dame, IN: Ave Maria, 1989.

Tozer, A. W. *The Pursuit of God.* Harrisburg, PA: Christian Publications, 1982.

Woolman, John. *The Journal and Major Essays of John Woolman.* Richmond, IN: Friends United Press, 1989.

Index of Scriptures

Index of Names and Subjects

What Is Renovaré?

Renovaré (from the Latin meaning "to renew") is an infrachurch movement committed to the renewal of the Church of Jesus Christ in all its multifaceted expressions. Founded by best-selling author Richard J. Foster, Renovaré is Christian in commitment, international in scope, and ecumenical in breadth.

In *The Renovaré Spiritual Formation Bible*, we observe how God spiritually formed his people through historical events and the practice of Spiritual Disciplines that is the with-God Life. Renovaré continues this emphasis on spiritual formation by placing it within the context of the two-thousand-year history of the Church and six great Christian traditions we find in its life—Contemplative: The Prayer-Filled Life; Holiness: The Virtuous Life; Charismatic: The Spirit-Empowered Life; Social Justice: The Compassionate Life; Evangelical: The Word-Centered Life; and Incarnational: The Sacramental Life. This balanced vision of Christian faith and witness was modeled for us by Jesus Christ and was evident in the lives of countless saints: Anthony, Francis of Assisi, Susanna Wesley, Phoebe Palmer, and others. The With-God Life of the People of God continues on today as Christians participate in the life and practices of local churches and look forward to spending eternity in that "all-inclusive community of loving persons with God at the very center of this community as its prime Sustainer and most glorious Inhabitant."

In addition to offering a balanced vision of the spiritual life, RENOVARÉ promotes a practical strategy for people seeking renewal by helping facilitate small spiritual formation groups; national, regional, and local conferences; one-day seminars; personal and group retreats; and readings from devotional classics that can sustain a long-term commitment to renewal. RENOVARÉ Resources for Spiritual Renewal, Spiritual Formation Guides, and *The Renovaré Spiritual Formation Bible*—books published by HarperOne—seek to integrate historical, scholarly, and inspirational materials into practical, readable formats. These resources can be used in a variety of settings, including small groups, private and organizational retreats, individual devotions, and church school classes. Written and edited by people committed to the renewal of the Church, all of the materials present a balanced vision of Christian life and faith coupled with a practical strategy for spiritual growth and enrichment.

For more information about RENOVARÉ and its mission, please log on to its Web site (www.renovare.org) or write RENOVARÉ, 8 Inverness Drive East, Suite 102, Englewood, CO 80112-5624, USA.